100
Cross-curricular
Maths
Lessons

David & Penny Glover

Years 1 & 2

Scottish Primary 1–3

Authors
David Glover and Penny Glover

Editor
Joel Lane

Assistant Editor
David Sandford

Series Designer
Heather C Sanneh

Illustrations
Shirley Walker

Cover photography
© Photodisc, Inc

Text © Penny Glover and David Glover
© 2002 Scholastic Ltd

Designed using Adobe Pagemaker

Published by Scholastic Ltd, Villiers House,
Clarendon Avenue, Leamington Spa, Warwickshire CV32 5PR

Visit our website at www.scholastic.co.uk

Printed by Cromwell Press Ltd, Trowbridge

1 2 3 4 5 6 7 8 9 0   2 3 4 5 6 7 8 9 0 1

British Library Cataloguing-in-Publication Data A catalogue
record for this book is available from the British Library.

ISBN 0-439-01686-X

Acknowledgement
Extracts from the National Curriculum for England © Crown copyright
material is reproduced with the permission of the Controller of HMSO
and the Queen's Printer for Scotland.
Extracts from the National Numeracy Strategy *Framework For Teaching
Mathematics* © Crown copyright. Reproduced under the terms of HMSO
Guidance Note 8.

Contents

Year 2

Introduction

Few of us are pure mathematicians. Our mathematical skills are practical, not abstract. We use mathematics to compare prices as we shop, to make measurements for DIY projects and to follow recipes in the kitchen. Often, we are hardly aware of the maths skills we are using. However, children need to have the value and application of their mathematics in other school subjects, as well as in everyday life, made clear. Such realistic contexts broaden and develop their mathematical understanding and skills. For this reason, the National Numeracy Strategy and National Curriculum, and the Scottish National Guidelines on Mathematics 5–14, emphasise the importance of looking for links between mathematics and other curriculum areas.

The *100 Cross-curricular Maths Lessons* series presents lesson plans linking objectives from the National Numeracy Strategy to objectives in other subjects. The lessons are intended to take place during your numeracy time, but the mathematics is set in a cross-curricular context.

Each book in this series provides content for the daily maths lessons of two year groups. This book supports Years 1 and 2. The materials presented here can be used to substitute or supplement your daily maths lessons. The organisation of the mathematical objectives covered by the lesson plans follows the term-by-term sequence of topics set out in the National Numeracy Strategy's *Framework for Teaching Mathematics* (March 1999). Their content is also appropriate for, and adaptable to, the requirements of Primary 1–3 in Scottish schools. In Scotland, and in schools elsewhere that have decided not to adopt the National Numeracy Strategy, it will be necessary to choose activities to match your planning. To help you with this, reference grids listing the lessons' objectives are provided for each year group (see pages 16–18 and 94–6), together with a comprehensive index of maths topics and cross-curricular content on pages 175 and 176.

These lesson plans offer ideal additional or alternative activities to the main teaching activities given in the lesson plans of *100 Maths Lessons: Year 1* or *Year 2*, also published by Scholastic.

In Year 1 (Primary 2), children should be counting, reading, writing and ordering numbers to 20. They should be able to add, subtract, double and halve numbers to 10, and then to 20. They should also be taking their first steps in the measurement of length, mass and capacity, and beginning to work with simple 3-D and 2-D shapes. In Year 2 (Primary 3), the children should extend their knowledge of numbers to 100 and beyond. They should develop their addition and subtraction skills, and begin to multiply. They should also start to make measurements using standard units, and read scales to the nearest division. Their knowledge of shapes should develop such that they can describe shapes and their features, using the correct mathematical names. Finally, they should practise problem-solving skills in a variety of contexts, and begin to explain how they have solved problems.

The lessons in this book are planned to support this progression of mathematical knowledge and skills, with activities designed to match the children's developing abilities. Each lesson presents a mathematical challenge in the context of work in another subject, thus developing the child's knowledge and skills in that subject area also.

Using this book

The materials

This book provides 50 cross-curricular maths lessons for Year 1 and 50 for Year 2. Each lesson plan sets out its numeracy objectives and objectives for another curriculum subject or subjects. The intention is that the mathematics is developed in a context that links strongly to another subject area, simultaneously fulfilling the linked subject objectives. Photocopiable activity sheets and assessment activities support the lesson plans for each term.

Organisation

This book follows the Year 1 and Year 2 topic plans given in the National Numeracy Strategy's *Framework for Teaching Mathematics*. Complete planning grids for both years are set out on pages 16–18 for Year 1 and 94–6 for Year 2.

An extract from the planning grid for Year 1 is reproduced overleaf. Columns 1 and 2 list the National Numeracy Strategy unit numbers and topics. Column 3 gives the numeracy objective(s) to be met by the lesson plan.

Term 1	Topics	Maths objectives	Cross-curricular objectives	Activities
Unit 1	Counting and properties of numbers	Know the number names, and recite them in order to at least 20, from and back to zero.	**Literacy** Read on sight high-frequency words and other familiar words.	**p.19: Number cards** Read and write number vocabulary using flash cards.
2–4	Place value and ordering Understanding + and – Mental calculation strategies (+ and –) Money and 'real-life' problems Making decisions and checking results	Understand and use the vocabulary of comparing and ordering numbers, including ordinal numbers to at least 20. Order numbers to at least 20, and position them on a number track. Count in twos and fives. Understand the operation of addition. Begin to recognise that more than two numbers can be added together. Use mental strategies to solve simple problems set in 'real-life', money or measurement contexts. Choose and use appropriate number operations and mental strategies to solve problems.	**Geography** Observe and record [eg identify buildings in the street and complete a chart]. Make observations about where things are located. Links to QCA Geography Unit 1. **PE** Develop skills for simple games. Apply rules and conventions for different activities. Links to QCA PE Games activities Unit 1. **D&T** Design and make artefacts using a range of materials. **Art** Investigate how colour and pattern can be combined and organised for different purposes.	**p.20: House numbers** Make model street with numbered houses. Address and deliver letters to correct house. **p.21: Keeping score** Devise simple games in which different numbers of points are scored for different achievements. **p.22: Class stall** Design and make items to sell on class stall at school fair. Match coins to prices. **p.23: Football shirts** Investigate the number of ways of colouring the stripes on a football shirt with three colours.
5–6	Measures – including problems Shape and space Reasoning about shapes	Understand and use the vocabulary related to length, mass and capacity. Use everyday language to describe features of familiar 3-D and 2-D shapes. Use everyday language to describe position, direction and movement. Talk about things that turn. Make whole turns and half turns. Use everyday language to describe familiar features of 2-D shapes including... triangle, square, rectangle..., referring to properties such as the shapes of flat faces, or the number of faces or corners... or the number and types of sides. Make and describe models, patterns and pictures using construction kits, everyday materials. Investigate a general statement about familiar numbers or shapes by finding examples that satisfy it.	**Science** To make and record observations and measurements. To recognise similarities and differences between living things. Links to QCA Science Unit 1A. **PE** Create and perform dances using a range of movement patterns. Create and perform fluent sequences on the floor and using apparatus. Links to QCA PE Dance activities Unit 1. **Art** Explore visual elements including colour, pattern, shape and form. Working on their own, and collaborating with others, on projects in two and three dimensions and on different scales using a range of materials and processes. Links with QCA Art Unit 1C.	**p.24: Animal records** Compare records from the animal kingdom. Which is the tallest animal? Which is the most massive? **p.25: Moving shapes** Move around the hall in the manner of 3-D shapes: rolling and sliding. Make 3-D and 2-D shapes with their bodies and in groups. **p.26: Tangrams** Use basic shapes cut from card to make pictures (tangrams).
7	Asse...			p.35.

The cross-curricular objectives are set out in column 4 together with links to relevant units in the QCA's primary schemes of work. The lesson titles, with brief descriptions of their content, are listed in column 5.

Lesson plans

Each of the lesson plans contains the following sections:

Objectives
The numeracy and cross-curricular subject objectives are stated, together with links to relevant QCA schemes of work.

Vocabulary
The vocabulary sections have drawn on the National Numeracy Strategy's *Mathematical Vocabulary* booklet. New or specific maths vocabulary to be used during the lesson is listed. Use this vocabulary with the whole class, so that all the children have a chance to hear it in context and understand it. Encourage the children to use the vocabulary orally, when asking or answering questions, so that they develop understanding of its mathematical meaning.

Resources
The resources required for the lesson are listed.

Background
Key maths strategies, skills or operations relevant to the specific lesson are outlined, and the cross-curricular context is introduced. This section may provide useful background for the lesson, such as historical facts or science explanations.

Preparation
Preparation needed in advance of the lesson is highlighted – for example, assembling materials, making resources or photocopying pages.

Main teaching activity
This explains what the teacher should do in the whole-class teaching session, lasting about 30 minutes. In some lessons, much of the time will be spent in whole-class interactive teaching. In others, the whole-class session will be shorter, with practical or paper-based activities being provided for groups, pairs or individuals.

Differentiation
This section suggests adaptations and extensions to the main teaching activity in order to meet the needs of less able and more able children within your class.

Plenary
This section is an opportunity to bring the

children back together for a concluding whole-class session. It offers opportunities to review and reinforce key ideas, compare strategies and outcomes, develop the cross-curricular links and assess the children's progress.

Planning and organisation

These lesson plans do *not* form a self-contained mathematics course. Rather, they are designed to be integrated into your overall scheme of work for mathematics and, more generally, to be linked to your plans for other subject areas. The grids on pages 16–18 and 94–6 are the best starting point for deciding how these lessons can be incorporated into your teaching.

Assessment

Three termly assessment activity sheets, together with supporting notes (including practical assessment opportunities) are included with each year's lesson plans. These can be incorporated into your assessment strategy for mathematics.

The assessment activity sheets are designed to introduce children to the style of questions found in the national tests. They are set in cross-curricular contexts drawn from the preceding term's lessons. Three activities are included on each assessment sheet. It is not essential for  the children to have had experience of these particular contexts; but it is important that they are comfortable with using their maths in a variety of less obviously mathematical situations. More able children will probably complete the exercises with minimal guidance. Most children, however, will need considerable support the first few times they tackle this type of activity.

Practical assessment tasks are also of great value in making a judgement of a child's progress, particularly for less able children who find formal paper-and- pencil activities demanding. A suggestion for a practical assessment task has been included in each assessment lesson. Set selected children to complete the practical task while the rest of the class work on the paper-based activities. Review the answers as a class. Collect the completed activity sheets, and make notes on your observations of the practical work, to use as an aid to judging individual children's progress and to include in your records.

Resources
Photocopiable sheets

These sheets support individual lessons, and may be copied for distribution to your class. Some sheets (pages A–G) serve as more general resources that have applications in more than one lesson (for example, ordinal numbers, days of the week, months and seasons). These sheets can be copied onto or backed with thin card before being cut up. They may be laminated to produce more durable resources.

Classroom equipment

All the equipment used in this book will normally be found in any primary school. The following list gives items that will be needed on a regular basis:

● A flip chart and marker pens (and/or a whiteboard or chalkboard)
● Sets of numeral flash cards 0–100
● Counting apparatus (such as counters, sorting toys, wooden cubes, beads and laces)
● Measuring apparatus, including centimetre rulers, tape measures, measuring jugs and a classroom balance
● Craft or technology materials and tools – scissors, glue, adhesive tape, card, dowel, modelling clay, construction kits and so on
● Shapes, including 2-D and 3-D shapes
● Safety mirrors
● Art materials
● Coins, real and plastic
● Dice
● Large analogue and digital clock faces
● Programmable robots (Roamer or PIP)
● Dominoes
● Recyclable materials, including card boxes and plastic containers
● Musical instruments
● PE apparatus – beanbags, hoops and balls

ICT

A number of the activities are computer based. These activities require a computer program with text and drawing capabilities such as *Textease* (Softease Ltd) or *Microsoft Word*. There are many equivalent programs in use that allow children to enter and edit text, and to create and manipulate geometrical shapes on the same page. Use a program with which you are familiar, and check that you can produce the desired outcome with confidence before setting children to work on the activity.

These activities will be greatly enhanced if the computer is connected to a printer on which the children can print their work for subsequent discussion and display.

Number words zero to one hundred (1)

zero	one	two
three	four	five
six	seven	eight
nine	ten	eleven
twelve	thirteen	fourteen
fifteen	sixteen	seventeen
eighteen	nineteen	twenty
twenty-one	twenty-two	twenty-three

Number words zero to one hundred (2)

twenty-four	twenty-five	twenty-six
twenty-seven	twenty-eight	twenty-nine
thirty	thirty-one	thirty-two
thirty-three	thirty-four	thirty-five
thirty-six	thirty-seven	thirty-eight
thirty-nine	forty	forty-one
forty-two	forty-three	forty-four
forty-five	forty-six	forty-seven
forty-eight	forty-nine	fifty

Number words zero to one hundred (3)

fifty-one	fifty-two	fifty-three
fifty-four	fifty-five	fifty-six
fifty-seven	fifty-eight	fifty-nine
sixty	sixty-one	sixty-two
sixty-three	sixty-four	sixty-five
sixty-six	sixty-seven	sixty-eight
sixty-nine	seventy	seventy-one
seventy-two	seventy-three	seventy-four
seventy-five	seventy-six	seventy-seven

Number words zero to one hundred (4)

seventy-eight	seventy-nine	eighty
eighty-one	eighty-two	eighty-three
eighty-four	eighty-five	eighty-six
eighty-seven	eighty-eight	eighty-nine
ninety	ninety-one	ninety-two
ninety-three	ninety-four	ninety-five
ninety-six	ninety-seven	ninety-eight
ninety-nine	one hundred	

Days, months and seasons

Monday	Tuesday	Wednesday
Thursday	Friday	Saturday
Sunday	January	February
March	April	May
June	July	August
September	October	November
December	Winter	Spring
Summer	Autumn	

Ordinal numbers

1st	2nd	3rd
4th	5th	6th
7th	8th	9th
10th	11th	12th
13th	14th	15th
16th	17th	18th
19th	20th	

Ordinal number words

first	second	third
fourth	fifth	sixth
seventh	eighth	ninth
tenth	eleventh	twelfth
thirteenth	fourteenth	fifteenth
sixteenth	seventeenth	eighteenth
nineteenth	twentieth	

100
Cross-curricular
Maths
Lessons

Lesson plans and photocopiable activity pages

Year 1

YEAR 1

Term 1	Topics	Maths objectives	Cross-curricular objectives	Activities
Unit 1	Counting and properties of numbers	Know the number names, and recite them in order to at least 20, from and back to zero.	**Literacy** Read on sight high-frequency words and other familiar words.	**p.19: Number cards** Read and write number vocabulary using flash cards.
2–4	Place value and ordering	Understand and use the vocabulary of comparing and ordering numbers, including ordinal numbers to at least 20. Order numbers to at least 20, and position them on a number track.	**Geography** Observe and record [eg identify buildings in the street and complete a chart]. Make observations about where things are located. Links to QCA Geography Unit 1.	**p.20: House numbers** Make model street with numbered houses. Address and deliver letters to correct house.
	Understanding + and –			
	Mental calculation strategies (+ and –)	Count in twos and fives. Understand the operation of addition. Begin to recognise that more than two numbers can be added together.	**PE** Develop skills for simple games. Apply rules and conventions for different activities. Links to QCA PE Games activities Unit 1.	**p.21: Keeping score** Devise simple games in which different numbers of points are scored for different achievements.
	Money and 'real-life' problems	Use mental strategies to solve simple problems set in 'real-life', money or measurement contexts.	**D&T** Design and make artefacts using a range of materials.	**p.22: Class stall** Design and make items to sell on class stall at school fair. Match coins to prices.
	Making decisions and checking results	Choose and use appropriate number operations and mental strategies to solve problems.	**Art** Investigate how colour and pattern can be combined and organised for different purposes.	**p.23: Football shirts** Investigate the number of ways of colouring the stripes on a football shirt with three colours.
5–6	Measures – including problems	Understand and use the vocabulary related to length, mass and capacity.	**Science** To make and record observations and measurements. To recognise similarities and differences between living things. Links to QCA Science Unit 1A.	**p.24: Animal records** Compare records from the animal kingdom. Which is the tallest animal? Which is the most massive?
	Shape and space			
	Reasoning about shapes	Use everyday language to describe features of familiar 3-D and 2-D shapes. Use everyday language to describe position, direction and movement. Talk about things that turn. Make whole turns and half turns.	**PE** Create and perform dances using a range of movement patterns. Create and perform fluent sequences on the floor and using apparatus. Links to QCA PE Dance activities Unit 1.	**p.25: Moving shapes** Move around the hall in the manner of 3-D shapes: rolling and sliding. Make 3-D and 2-D shapes with their bodies and in groups.
		Use everyday language to describe familiar features of 2-D shapes including... triangle, square, rectangle..., referring to properties such as the shapes of flat faces, or the number of faces or corners... or the number and types of sides. Make and describe models, patterns and pictures using construction kits, everyday materials. Investigate a general statement about familiar numbers or shapes by finding examples that satisfy it.	**Art** Explore visual elements including colour, pattern, shape and form. Working on their own, and collaborating with others, on projects in two and three dimensions and on different scales using a range of materials and processes. Links with QCA Art Unit 1C.	**p.26: Tangrams** Use basic shapes cut from card to make pictures (tangrams).
7	Assess and review			See p.35.
8	Counting and the properties of numbers	Count on and back in ones from any small number, and in tens from and back to zero. Count on in twos from zero, then one, and begin to recognise odd or even numbers to about 20 as 'every other number'; count in steps of five from zero to 20 or more, then back again; and begin to count on in steps of three from zero.	**Music** To explore musical patterns. To listen with concentration. Links with QCA Music Unit 4.	**p.27: Counting rhythms** Clapping and counting rhythms.
	Reasoning about numbers			
9–11	Place value, ordering, estimating	Know by heart all pairs of numbers with a total of ten. Addition facts for all pairs of numbers with a total of up to at least five, and corresponding subtraction facts. Use mental strategies to solve simple problems set in 'real-life'... explaining methods and reasoning orally.	**Literacy** Non-fiction writing – to write simple questions.	**p.28: Story problems** Write 'story' problems for other children to solve– Lisa has 5 pens and Tim has 2 pens. How many more pens has Lisa than Tim?
	Understanding + and–	Begin to know what each digit in a two-digit number represents. Partition a 'teens' number and begin to partition larger two digit numbers into a multiple of 10 and ones (TU).	**Art and design** Be taught about: Visual elements including colour and pattern. Materials and processes used in making art, craft and design. Links to QCA Art Unit 1B.	**p.29: Number necklaces** Make bead necklaces, grouping beads in tens and ones.
	Mental calculation strategies (+ and –)			
	Money and 'real-life' problems	Understand the operation of addition, and of subtraction... and use the related vocabulary.	**Science** Recognise and compare the main external parts of the bodies of humans and other animals. Links to QCA Science Unit 1A.	**p.30: Arms, legs, fingers and toes** Counting, addition and subtraction games with fingers, toes etc.
	Making decisions	Count on and back in ones from any small number. Understand the operation of addition, and of subtraction, and use the related vocabulary. Begin to know addition facts for all pairs of numbers with a total up to at least 10, and corresponding subtraction facts.	**Literacy** Reading comprehension – to read and follow simple instructions.	**p.31: Number ladder** Play a number game based on a 0–20 number ladder.
		Use mental strategies to solve simple problems set in 'real-life', money or measurement contexts.	**Literacy** To write and draw simple labels and instructions for everyday classroom use.	**p.32: Shopping** Write price labels and role-play shopping transactions.
12–13	Measures and time, including problems	Understand and use the vocabulary related to time. Order familiar events in time. Know the days of the week.	**Literacy** To read on sight high-frequency words including days of the week. To read/recite familiar stories and rhymes. To use rhymes and patterned stories as models for their own writing.	**p.33: Days of the week 1** Explore poems and rhymes based on the days of the week.
	Organising and using data	Solve a given problem by sorting, classifying and organising information in simple ways, such as: using objects or pictures; in a list or simple table.	**Science** Learn that there are different ways of making sounds... **Music** Be taught how sounds can be made in different ways... Links to QCA Science Unit 1F, Music Unit 2.	**p.34 Musical instruments** Sort the school musical instruments into wind, string and percussion instruments. Record the sort.
14	Assess and review			**p.35: Assessment 1**

100 CROSS-CURRICULAR MATHS LESSONS Years 1 & 2/Scottish Primary 1–3

YEAR 1

Term 2	Topics	Maths objectives	Cross-curricular objectives	Activities
1	Counting and properties of numbers	Know the number names and recite them in order to at least 20, from and back to zero... Count on in twos from zero, then one, and begin to recognise odd and even numbers...	**Literacy** Learn and recite simple poems and rhymes, with actions, and reread them from the text. Identify patterns of rhythm, rhyme and sounds in poems and their effects. **Music** Use their voices expressively by singing songs and speaking chants and rhymes. Links to QCA Music Unit 1.	**p.36: Number songs and rhymes** Learn number songs and rhymes, eg 'The animals went in two by two...' Act them out with counting games.
2–4	Place value and ordering Understanding + and − Mental calculation strategies (+ and −) Money and 'real-life' problems Making decisions	Read and write numerals from zero to at least 20. Order numbers to at least 20, and position them on a number track.	**ICT** Be taught how to plan and give instructions to make things happen. Be taught to present their completed work effectively. Explore a variety of ICT tools. Links to QCA IT Unit 1A.	**p.37: Dot-to-dot** Complete a dot-to-dot picture. Design and make their own dot-to-dot pictures using a computer drawing package.
		Begin to know: addition facts for all pairs of numbers with a total up to at least 10, and the corresponding subtraction facts. Use everyday language to describe features of familiar 3-D shapes. Make and describe models. Begin to relate solid shapes to pictures of them.	**Design and technology** Measure, mark out, cut and shape a range of materials. Assemble, join and combine materials and components. Links to QCA D&T Units 1A, 1B and 1D.	**p.38: Home-made dice** Make and use card dice.
		Understand and use the vocabulary of estimation. Give a sensible estimate of a number of objects that can be checked by counting (up to about 30 objects).	**Science** Group living things according to observable similarities and differences.. Links to QCA Science Unit 2C.	**p.39: How many minibeasts?** Estimate the number of minibeasts in a group, then count to check.
		Solve simple problems set in real-life money and measurement contexts. Find totals and change from up to 20p. Measure mass using non–standard units.	**Geography** Understand that a variety of features and facilities form part of their local area. Links to QCA Geography Unit 1. **Science** Make and record measurements.	**p.40: Postage stamps** Make and 'sell' home-made stamps for letters and parcels to be delivered around the school.
		Understand the operation of addition and the related vocabulary. Understand and use in practical contexts: more, add, sum, total, altogether, equals, sign... and read and write the plus (+) and equals (=) signs.	**Literacy** To understand, read and make collections of significant words linked to particular topics.	**p.41: Addition words** Formulate number sentences with addition word cards.
5–6	Measures – including problems Shape and space Reasoning about shapes	Measure and compare by direct (side by side) comparison.	**ICT** That objects can be compared and ordered according to criteria. Links to QCA ICT Unit 1D. **Science** Make simple comparisons and identify simple patterns.	**p.42: Compare and order** Compare children and objects by sequencing them according to height, length and mass.
		Make and describe patterns.	**Art and design** Learn about visual elements including pattern and shape.	**p.43: Shape patterns** Recognise, describe and create repeating patterns of basic shapes.
		Make shapes and patterns with increasing accuracy, and describe their features. Begin to recognise line symmetry.	**Art and design** Learn about visual elements including pattern and shape. Links to QCA Art Unit 1.	**p.44: Fold in half** Investigate the symmetry of shapes by cutting out and folding.
7	Assess and review			See p.46.
8	Counting and the properties of numbers Reasoning about numbers	Describe and extend number sequences: count on and back in ones from any small number, and in tens from and back to zero; count on in twos from 0, then 1, and begin to recognise odd or even numbers to about 20 as 'every other number'; count in steps of 5 from 0 to 20 or more, then back again; begin to count on in steps of 3 from 0.	**PE** Perform basic skills in travelling and being still, on the floor and using apparatus. Links to QCA PE Gymnastic activities Unit 1.	**p.47: Number track** Counting games and activities based on a playground number track.
9–10	Understanding + and − Mental calculation strategies (+ and −) Money and 'real-life' problems Making decisions	Read the time to the hour or half hour on analogue clocks.	**Literacy** To read and recite a variety of poems, songs and stories on similar themes (in this case 'Time').	**p.46: What's the time, Mr Wolf?** Learn songs and rhymes based on time. Play time-based games.
		Solve mathematical problems or puzzles, recognise simple patterns and relationships, generalise and predict.	**History** Identify a wide range of differences between old and new toys; give some reasons for these differences; extend the ability to use everyday words connected with the passage of time. Links to QCA History Unit 1.	**p.47: Dominoes** Number sorting, sequencing and matching activities with dominoes.
		Solve mathematical problems or puzzles, recognise simple patterns and relationships, generalise and predict.	**Geography** Identify and describe what places are like. Identify and describe where places are. Recognise how places compare with other places. Links to QCA Geography Unit 1.	**p.48: Postcard puzzles** Make puzzles with photographs and pictures of the local environment.
		Recognise coins and notes of different values. Solve simple word problems involving money and explain how the problem was solved.	**Geography** Observe features of the local environment. Links to QCA Geography Unit 1.	**p.49: Giving change** Role-play asking for and receiving change in local shops and other locations.
		Recognise coins of different values. Solve simple word problems involving money...	**Design and technology** Design and make assignments using a range of materials. Links to QCA Design and Technology Unit 1C.	**p.50: Fill your basket** Make and play a 'Fill your basket' shopping game.
11–12	Measures and time, including problems Organising and using data	Understand and use the vocabulary related to time; know and use units of time and relationships between them; read the time from a clock; solve problems involving time, and explain how the problem was solved.	**Literacy** Read high-frequency words including the days of the week. **History** Place events in chronological order.	**p.51: My timetable** Make a personal time table to show the getting-up time, mealtimes and bedtime.
		Solve a problem by sorting, classifying and organising information in simple ways, such as: using objects or pictures; in a list or simple table. Discuss and explain results.	**Science** Learn that there are different ways of making sound. **Music** Be taught how sounds can be made in different ways. Links to QCA Science Unit 1F, Music Unit 2.	**p.52: 'I can play the...'** Conduct a class survey of favourite instruments. Present results as a block graph.
Unit 13	Assess and review			p.53: Assessment 2

Term 3	Topics	Maths objectives	Cross-curricular objectives	Activities
1	Counting and properties of numbers Place value and ordering	Know the number names and recite them in order to at least 20, from and back to zero. Read and write numerals from 0 to at least 20. Solve a given problem by sorting, classifying and organising information in simple ways.	**Literacy** Sound and name letters of the alphabet. To know alphabetic order.	**p.54: Secret codes** Use alphabet codes. What is the twelfth letter of the alphabet?
2–4	Understanding + and – Mental calculation strategies (+ and –) Money and 'real-life' problems Making decisions	Know the number names and recite them in order to at least 20, from and back to zero.	**History** To place events and objects in chronological order. To find out about the past from a range of sources of information. To ask and answer questions about the past.	**p.55: My history book** Make a simple 'history' book for the past twenty years on a favourite topic.
		Use everyday language to describe position, direction and movement. Talk about things that turn. Make whole turns and half turns.	**PE** Remember and repeat simple skills and actions with increasing control and co-ordination. **ICT** To plan and give instructions to make things happen. Links to QCA Information technology Unit 1F.	**p.56: Playground robots** Role-play programmable robots.
		Know by heart addition doubles of all numbers to at least five. Identify near doubles, using doubles already known. Use mental strategies to solve simple problems... using doubling... explaining methods and reasoning orally.	**English** To take turns to speak, sharing ideas and organising what they say.	**p.57: Doubles and near doubles** Discuss mental calculation strategies involving doubles and near doubles.
5–6	Measures – including problems Shape and space Reasoning about shapes	Use everyday language to describe position, direction and movement.	**Geography** Identify and describe where places are. Make maps and plans (for example, a pictorial map of a place in the story).	**p.58: Treasure Island** Play a game in a sand tray to find hidden treasure. Develop vocabulary of position and movement.
		Compare two capacities by direct comparison; extend to more than two. Measure using uniform non-standard units. Record estimates and measurements as 'about three beakers full'.	**Science** Make and record observations and measurements.	**p.59: How much does it hold?** Compare the capacities of different containers using measures such as cupfuls.
		Use everyday language to describe features of familiar shapes including the circle... Use everyday language to describe position, direction and movement. Talk about things that turn. Make whole turns and half turns.	**PE** Use movement imaginatively... performing basic skills (for example, travelling, being still, making a shape, jumping, turning and gesturing). Links to QCA PE Dance activities Unit 1.	**p.60: Circle dance** Explore circles and turns in PE. **p.61: Shape spotting** Explore shapes in the local environment – triangular signs, round windows, cylindrical bins...
7	Assess and review			See p.68.
8	Counting and the properties of numbers Reasoning about numbers	Understand and use the vocabulary of estimation. Give a sensible estimate of a number of objects that can be checked by counting (eg up to about 30 objects).	**Literacy** To learn new words from reading and shared experiences, and make collections of words linked to particular topics.	**p.62: How many animals?** Estimate numbers of toy animals, then count to check. How many cows? How many pigs? Introduce collective nouns: herd, flock...
9–11	Place value, ordering, estimating Understanding + and – Mental calculation strategies (+ and –) Money and 'real-life' problems	Order numbers to at least 20, and position them on a number track. Understand and use the vocabulary related to time. Order familiar events in time.	**History** Place events in chronological order. Use common words and phrases relating to the passage of time.	**p.63: Time of day** Mark events on a timeline for one day.
		Understand and use the vocabulary of comparing and ordering numbers. Understand the operation of addition, and of subtraction, and use the related vocabulary.	**ICT** Explore a variety of ICT tools. Be taught how to plan and give instructions to make things happen. Links to QCA IT Unit 1F.	**p.64: Robot run** Program a floor robot to move and change direction along a number line.
		Recognise coins of different values. Find totals and change from up to 20p. Work out how to pay an exact sum using smaller coins.	**Design and technology** Investigate and evaluate a range of familiar products. Design and make assignments using a range of materials.	**p.65: Slot machine** Make, label and operate 'slot machines' for purchasing tickets/drinks.
12–13	Making decisions Measures, and time, including problems Organising and using data	Use mental strategies to solve simple problems set in real-life contexts. Compare two lengths by direct comparison. Solve a given problem by sorting, classifying and organising information in simple ways.	**Literacy** To know alphabetic order. To recognise the structure and conventions of books.	**p.66: Library books** Investigate ways of organising books in the library: size, fiction/non-fiction, alphabetical order...
		Measure using uniform non-standard units.	**Science** To recognise and compare the main external parts of the bodies of humans. Links to QCA Science Unit 1A.	**p.67: My measuring scale** Discuss and use measurement units based on body parts.
14	Assess and review			p.68: Assessment 3

Linked to Literacy

1 Number cards

Background

Most children will be reading number symbols and names to ten confidently at the end of the Reception year. Many will be starting to recognise and use symbols and number names to 20 and beyond. This lesson uses flash cards to practise and reinforce children's on-sight recognition of number symbols and number words to 20. It links to word- level work in literacy.

The number names beyond ten – eleven, twelve and the 'teen' numbers – are initially unfamiliar, and mistakes will at first be frequent. However, with daily counting practice, the introduction of reading books and posters that include number names to twenty, and classroom displays of number symbols and words, these words will soon become as familiar as the number names to ten.

Preparation

Set out the counting objects ready for a whole-class introduction. Put a set of numeral cards and a set of number name cards on each desk for the group activity.

Main teaching activity

Use a set of 20 objects to practise counting to 20 with the whole class. Count from 0 to 20 and back again. Count again, this time holding up the numeral flash cards as you do so. Repeat using the number word flash cards. Finally, play a game in which you shuffle the numeral cards and number word cards and pick one at random. The children must

say the number name as you flash each card.

The children now return to their desks and work in groups with the sets of cards.
● Shuffle the set of numeral cards and ask each group to arrange them in order.
● Shuffle the number words and ask each group to match them to the number symbols.
● Use the cards to play a game of 'pick-a-pair'. Shuffle both packs and spread them face-down across the table. The children take turns to turn over a card, read the numeral or word on it, then turn over a second card. If the two cards make a pair, they keep them. If not, they are turned back over. The children will recall where the individual cards are, so their success rate in 'picking pairs' will increase as the game proceeds.

Differentiation

Stretch more able children by introducing numbers beyond 20 into the pick-a-pair game, for example 30, 40, 50... 100.

Less able children should concentrate on the numbers 0 to 10 until they are reading the numerals and words confidently.

Plenary

Conclude the lesson with a game in which you pick a pair of cards (numerals, number names or one of each) and hold them up. Ask the children *Which number is more?* or *Which number is less?*

Linked to
Geography

2 House numbers

Objectives

Numeracy
Understand and use the vocabulary of comparing and ordering numbers, including ordinal numbers to at least 20.
Order numbers to at least 20, and position them on a number track.

Geography
Observe and record (for example, identify buildings in the street and complete a chart).
Make observations about where things are located.
Links to QCA Geography Unit 1.

Resources

Cardboard boxes and other junk materials suitable for making model houses; adhesive, paints, scissors, felt pens and other resources as needed.

Vocabulary

the same number as
order
first, second, third...
last
before, after
next
between

Background

The numbers that we commonly think of as **ordinal numbers** are 'first', 'second', 'third' and so on. However, any number that we use in everyday life to locate an object or item in a sequence is an ordinal number: position in a race, page in a book, house in a street and so on. A **cardinal number** is always a quantity or total. So in the statement 'I live at 49 Gerbil Street', 49 is an ordinal number. But in the statement 'There are 54 houses in Gerbil Street', 54 is a cardinal number.

Most children in Year 1 will know the number of the house (or flat) they live in, and recognise that the houses along a street are numbered in sequence. House numbering is a significant feature of the children's local environment, since using these numbers is essential to finding a particular address. The children should know their own house (or flat) number as part of their growing awareness of how places in the local environment are located (for example, by someone delivering post).

Preparation

Set out the construction and art resources for a practical lesson. Cover tables and provide aprons according to your normal classroom practice.

Main teaching activity

Ask each child to make a model of a house in which he or she would like to live. The houses could be constructed from cardboard boxes, with film canisters as chimney-pots, cut-out windows and matchboxes as doorsteps – let the children use the materials imaginatively. (PVA medium in the paint will help it to stick to the plastic or glossy exteriors of some boxes; alternatively, such boxes can be taken apart and reconstructed inside-out.) When each child has completed and painted a house, make a street display. Ask the class to count the houses and number them in order, even numbers along one side of the street and odd numbers along the other side. Ask each child to find his or her house and remember its number. Label the houses with the children's names.

Finally, ask the children to write and address letters to their friends in 'Our Street'. Appoint a post-boy or post-girl to deliver the letters.

Differentiation

Challenge more able children to compile an ordered list of the actual house (or flat) numbers of the children in the class.

Less able children should concentrate on finding and reading the numbers of their own and friends' houses in the model street.

Plenary

Collect the delivered letters from the model street and distribute them to the children, discussing the addresses: *This letter is for Sophie at number 7, Our Street. At which end of the street does she live? Who is her next-door neighbour at number 9? Does she live nearer to number 6 or number 12? Who lives at the first house in the street? Who lives at the fifth house? Who lives next to number 10?...*

Linked to
P E

3 Keeping score

Objectives

Numeracy
Count in twos and fives.
Understand the operation of addition.
Begin to recognise that more than two numbers can be added together.
PE
Develop skills for simple games.
Apply rules and conventions for different activities.
Links to QCA PE Games activities, Unit 1.

Resources

Beanbags, hoops, balls and/or other PE apparatus as required; a number line on a board or flip chart; blank cards, a marker pen.

Vocabulary

add
more
plus
sum
total
altogether
score
one more, two more... ten more

Background

Counting on in ones, twos, threes and fives are important skills for developing mental addition strategies. People who regularly add up numbers in lists, such as fruit and vegetable prices on a market stall or scores in games of darts or cricket, soon become adept at mental addition. In the same way, keeping score during games in PE provides an excellent context in which children can develop and practise their addition skills.

Preparation

In advance of this lesson, the children should have practised counting together from 0 to 20 in ones, twos, threes and fives.

Main teaching activity

In a PE lesson outdoors or in a hall, ask the children to help you devise a simple game in which they score points each time an action is performed or a goal scored. A possible example is the beanbag target game illustrated below.

Divide the children into teams of six.

Arrange some different-sized hoops in a pattern on the ground. Assign a score to each size of hoop (for example, large hoops could score 2 and small hoops 5).

Write the scores on cards and place them in the hoops. Stand each team in turn behind a line a suitable distance from the pattern. Each member of the team throws a beanbag towards the hoops. When all six bags have landed, add up the total score as a class. Use the number line to help the children add by counting on. Write the teams' scores on the board or flip chart.

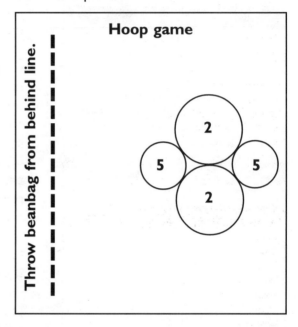

Hoop game

Throw beanbag from behind line.

2

5   5

2

Differentiation

Ask groups of more able children to devise and play their own scoring games. In a follow-up lesson, they could write simple lists of rules for their games.

Less able children should concentrate on keeping score in simple games in which a fixed number of points (for example, two) is scored for each success. The first child to reach 20 is the winner.

Plenary

As a class, discuss the scoring systems used in games the children watch or play. Some children will know that in snooker, the different-coloured balls are worth different numbers of points. In football, each 'goal' scored counts as one point; but in basketball, scores are worth 2 or 3 points. In darts, the first player to reach 501 is the winner; in crazy golf, the player with the lowest score wins the game.

Linked to
D & T

4 Class stall

Objectives

Numeracy
Use mental strategies to solve simple problems set in 'real life', money or measurement contexts.

Design and technology
Design and make artefacts using a range of materials.

Resources

Sets of plastic coins for shopping role-play; materials to make items for sale (for example, the greetings cards and calendars shown in the illustration below require card, paints, coloured tissue paper, adhesive and glitter); examples of finished products of the type the children will be making.

Vocabulary

money
coin
penny, pence, pound
price
cost
buy
sale
spend, spent
change
dear
cheap
how much?
how many?
total

Background

Number work must be practised within real contexts in order for children to become proficient with calculations involving money, measurements and other everyday quantities. A class shop or a stall at the summer or autumn fair provide ideal opportunities for children to role-play or engage in real buying and selling transactions involving prices, coin values and change. Making and pricing suitable items for the stall involves the children in the design and technology process of making a product for a specific purpose.

Preparation

Set out the materials for a practical art or technology lesson, covering the tables and providing aprons according to your normal classroom practice.

Main teaching activity

Start the lesson with a class discussion of a stall for the school fair. Explain that the stall will be like a shop, and that the class must make items to sell in order to raise money. Ask them to suggest items to be sold, and discuss the prices that could be charged. Write a list on the board or flip chart: pencil 10p, plastic animal 20p, drink 15p and so on. Count out the coins needed to buy the different items. Role-play some simple shopping transactions, using questions such as: *You use a 20p coin to pay for a drink. How*

much change must I give you?'

Explain that you have decided that the children will make greetings cards and calendars (or other items you have selected) for the stall. Show them examples of finished products and discuss appropriate prices. Let the children work in groups to make the items. When they have completed their cards or calendars, they can take turns to role-play transactions in preparation for the school fair.

Differentiation

More able children could design and make their own items for sale. Ask them to discuss the relative values of their items and decide on prices.

Less able children should be given guidance on producing a simple greetings card. Help them to decide on a price and find the right coin or coins to pay for it.

Plenary

Set out the children's items on a display table and compile a price list. For example: Ask the class questions about possible

transactions: *How many small greetings cards can I buy for 10p? How much change will I get from 20p if I buy a small card and a large card? Which item is the cheapest? Which item is the most expensive? How much money would we raise if we sold everything on the table?*

Linked to
Art & design

5 Football shirts

Objectives

Numeracy
Choose and use appropriate mental strategies to solve problems.
Art and design
Design images and artefacts.
Be taught about colour and pattern.

Resources

Copies of photocopiable page 69; coloured pencils or felt-tip pens.

Vocabulary

pattern
puzzle
What could we try next?
How did you work it out?

Background

Tackling simple puzzles and investigations stimulates children's mathematical thinking. They should be given opportunities to investigate problems and puzzles involving sorting and combinations. For example: *Investigate different ways of putting seven shirts in three drawers. How many games must three teams play so that each team plays every other team?* Investigations involving patterns and colour also provide an opportunity for developing ideas in art and design. For example: *Which colours look good together? Which colour combinations show up best from a distance?*

Preparation

Make enough copies of photocopiable page 69 for each child to carry out the investigation. Set out these sheets with crayons or felt-tip pens before the lesson.

Main teaching activity

Introduce the lesson by discussing the colours of football shirts with the children. What colours do their favourite teams play in? Do they like shirts that are a single colour, or do they prefer stripes or squares? Explain that they have been given the job of designing new football shirts for local teams.

But there is a problem! They have only three colours, but six teams need shirts. Can they make six different designs on the worksheet with no more than two colours per shirt? How many different shirt designs can they make altogether?

Differentiation

Less able children should concentrate on producing six distinct designs on a single sheet. Encourage them to think of simple designs that they have seen.

More able children should attempt to discover systematically how many different designs can be made altogether, with the shirts being divided into two colours vertically, horizontally and diagonally. Encourage them to see that using each colour in two quarters of the shirt is more pleasing artistically (and easier to recognise) than using one colour in only one quarter.

Plenary

In the plenary session, display and count all the different designs that the children have found. Don't expect the children at this stage to find all the possible designs. Discuss how different designs can be found by colouring the shirts systematically – by selecting one colour and combining it with each of the other available colours in turn. Discuss what different designs can be made with two colours. Ask: *Which designs look similar, and so might be confusing when worn by the two teams in a match? Which designs contrast more strongly?*

In a follow-up lesson, children could 'dress' child-sized cut-outs in painted or collaged shirts representing the different designs.

Linked to
S c i e n c e

Animal records

Objectives

Numeracy
Understand and use the vocabulary related to length, mass and capacity.
Science
Collect evidence by making observations and measurements.
Group living things according to observable similarities and differences.
Links to QCA Science Unit 1A.

Resources

Copies of photocopiable page 70; an infant measuring rule with clearly marked divisions, a classroom balance, a tape measure; several different-sized toy animals.

Vocabulary

measure
size
compare
length
height
short
tall
taller
weigh
weight
balance
scales
heaviest

Background

Comparison is a good basis for introducing measurement concepts. Two animal toys can be compared by placing them side by side, or on either side of a balance. Simple comparisons such as this introduce the vocabulary of measurement: *Which is taller? Which is heavier?* Comparing a single toy to the divisions on a ruler, or the standard masses on a balance, develops the measurement process.

Comparison of animal dimensions and records is a motivating context for measurement work. It links well to science work – both to observation and measurement process skills and to knowledge of differences between living things.

Preparation

Make a copy of photocopiable page 70 for each child. Arrange the toy animals in a line, but not in order of size.

Main teaching activity

Introduce the lesson by comparing the toy animals. *Which is the tallest toy? Which is the heaviest toy?* Discuss with the children how the heights and masses of the different toys can be measured and compared. Use the measuring rule to sort the toys by height. Use the balancing scales to compare pairs of toys and sort them by mass. *Is the tallest toy*

the heaviest toy? Which is the longest toy?

Discuss real animals. Ask the children for the names of the tallest and heaviest land animals. *Are there bigger animals in the sea? What were the biggest land animals that ever lived?* Conclude the Main teaching activity by letting the children complete the activity sheet. They should match the animal record holders to their descriptions.

Differentiation

Most children should complete the matching activity. Ask more able children to use reference books to look up the heights and weights of giraffes, elephants and other record holders. Can they mark out a length on the floor with a tape measure equivalent to the height of a giraffe?

Give less able children a selection of the toys used in the introductory activity to sort by height and weight in order to reinforce their sorting skills.

Plenary

Review the answers to the activity sheet. The correct answers are: tallest land animal – giraffe; heaviest land animal – elephant; fastest land animal – cheetah; biggest land animal ever – dinosaur; biggest animal ever – blue whale. If any children have managed to measure out a giraffe's height, compare this to the height of a child. *How many children would have to stand on each other's shoulders to reach as high as a giraffe?*

7 Moving shapes

Objectives

Numeracy
Use everyday language to describe features of familiar 3-D and 2-D shapes.
Use everyday language to describe position, direction and movement.
Talk about things that turn.
Make whole turns and half turns.
PE
Create and perform dances using simple movement patterns.
Perform basic skills in travelling, being still, finding space and using it safely, both on the floor and using apparatus.
Links to QCA PE Dance activities Unit 1.

Resources

Plane and solid shapes to hold up during the PE lesson: circle, triangle, square, rectangle, sphere, cylinder, cube, cuboid.

Vocabulary

shape
pattern
curved
straight
round
corner
point
side
cube
pyramid
sphere
cone
circle
triangle
square
rectangle
star
roll
turn

Background

Children's knowledge of shape and space is developed through concrete experience of objects in their environment. The features and vocabulary of various mathematical shapes become familiar through work with pictures, models, containers and construction kits in the classroom. A PE lesson in the hall is a good opportunity to reinforce the vocabulary of shape and movement. The children will develop their movement and co-ordination skills as they make shapes with their own bodies, or form shapes and patterns in groups.

Preparation

The vocabulary and properties of shapes should have been introduced in previous numeracy lessons. Prepare for a PE lesson according to your normal practice.

Main teaching activity

Explain to the children that during this PE lesson, they are going to explore the shapes that they can make with their bodies and the ways in which these different shapes can move. For example, they could:
● make a circle with their arms
● draw a triangle in the air
● walk around an imaginary square
● roll up to make a sphere or ball shape
● roll on the floor like a cylinder or a cone
● raise their hands and spread their feet apart to make a pyramid shape
● dance in circles
● join with partners to make triangles, squares, rectangles, stars and circles
● balance on one foot like a triangle standing on one corner
● sit firmly on the ground like a cube.
Encourage the children to use the language of shape to describe what they have chosen to do. Can they add to each other's descriptions?

Differentiation

Ask groups of more able children to devise simple sequences in which they change from one shape to another – for example, triangle to circle to square to star.
Less able children could work in groups to make the basic shapes: square, circle and triangle.

Plenary

Ask individual children to demonstrate some of the shape patterns and movements they have devised. Can the other children name the shapes being made?

Linked to
Art & design

8 Tangrams

Background

Tangrams are ancient Chinese puzzles in which a square is divided into triangles, rectangles, parallelograms and smaller squares. These must be reassembled to make the original square. The pieces of the puzzle can also be used to make designs such as boats, flowers, houses and birds. Making and working with tangrams is an opportunity for children both to develop their mathematical knowledge of shapes and to develop their artistic skills by creating designs and patterns. They will practise copying, cutting, sticking and display techniques.

Preparation

Set out enough of the resources for each child to make a tangram. If you want the children's tangram puzzles to be durable (perhaps to take home), copy page 71 onto strong and/or laminated card. Make a large tangram puzzle from card.

Main teaching activity

Show the class the parts of the large tangram puzzle you have prepared. Ask them to name each shape as you hold it up. Remind them of the characteristic features of these shapes, counting their sides and corners together. Demonstrate how the

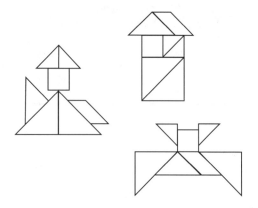

parts can be assembled into a square. (It is worth practising this before the lesson!) Explain that this puzzle is called a tangram and was popular in ancient China. Demonstrate how the parts can be used to make other designs, such as a boat.

Show the children the materials they will use to make their own puzzles. Set them working in pairs to colour and cut out the shapes. When the children have completed their puzzles, they can use the pieces to make various designs. They can also try to reassemble the original square. Explain that this is quite difficult, and they should not expect to succeed the first time. The children's patterns and designs can be glued to backing paper for classroom display.

Differentiation

All the children should be able to colour and cut out the tangram pieces. Ask less able children to concentrate on making new designs and shapes with their pieces. More able children can be challenged to reassemble the jumbled tangram pieces into a square. As an extension activity, they could design and make their own tangram puzzles from other starting shapes such as an equilateral triangle.

Plenary

Ask the children to help you display the designs they have created. Talk about each design, identifying how each shape has been used – for example, *Which shapes have been used to make the boat's sail?*

Linked to
M u s i c

9 Counting rhythms

Background

Counting only becomes second nature with regular practice. Counting in a variety of ways with the whole class should be a daily feature of numeracy lessons at this early stage. Children enjoy counting rhythmically when playing games such as hide-and-seek or skipping. Rhythmic counting helps children to develop the numeracy skill of counting in groups of two, three, five or ten. It can be encouraged and practised with the help of simple percussion instruments.

The ability to recognise and count regular rhythms, emphasising different beats, is an important musical skill. Links could also be made to the use of patterned stories and rhymes in literacy work (for example, in counting rhymes).

Main teaching activity

Clap or beat a regular rhythm. Start by counting every beat: *0, 1, 2, 3, 4...*
Ask the children to join in, chanting the numbers to the beat. Start from different numbers; count backwards and then forwards again. Now say the number corresponding only to every other beat: *0, –, 2, –, 4, –, 6, –...*
Emphasise the beats counted.
Count every third beat: *0, –, –, 3, –, –, 6, –, –, 9...* Experiment with rhythms and counting sequences including: odd numbers; even

numbers; counting in fives; counting from different starting numbers in ones, twos, threes and fives; counting in tens; counting forwards and backwards. With the children, use percussion instruments to accompany the rhythmic counting.

Differentiation

Ask less able children to count rhythmically on their own in ones and twos.
More able children can experiment on their own with counting in different intervals from different starting numbers.

Plenary

Play a game in which you beat out a rhythm with a regular emphasis: every other beat, every third beat, every fifth beat and so on. Ask the children to identify the intervals you are counting.

Linked to
L i t e r a c y

10 Story problems

Objectives

Numeracy
Know by heart: all pairs of numbers with a total of 10; addition facts for all pairs of numbers with a total up to at least 5, and the corresponding subtraction facts.
Use mental strategies to solve simple problems set in 'real life', explaining methods and reasoning orally.

Literacy
Non-fiction: write simple non-fiction texts.

Resources

Copies of photocopiable page 72, a 0–10 number line; unit cubes, pencils or other objects for counting.

Vocabulary

total
altogether
add
take away
problem

Background

This lesson is concerned with relating numbers to everyday problems. 'Story problems' are problems expressed in the language of an everyday context rather than as formally written arithmetic. For example, the problem 'Sophie has three pencils, Peter has two pencils. How many pencils do they have altogether?' is equivalent to the formal calculation 3 + 2 = 5. Children should practise solving story problems, explaining their reasoning orally.

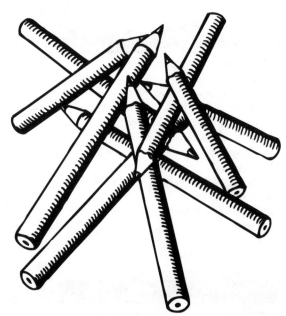

Creating their own story problems will help the children to build their understanding of the links between mathematics and objects in the real world. In the process, they will be developing their non-fiction writing skills by composing sentences in the form of questions, which end with a question mark rather than a full stop.

Preparation
Make one copy of page 72 for each child. Display the number line where it can be seen by the whole class.

Main teaching activity
Work through some story problems similar to those on page 72 with the whole class. Use the number line to add or take away by counting on or back. The children should then work individually on the photocopiable sheet, reading and answering the questions. When they are ready to write story problems of their own, discuss the technique as a class. Write a sum on the board (for

example, 3 + 2 = 5), and ask the children to illustrate it verbally by referring to real objects. They might suggest, for example: 'Three apples plus two apples makes five apples altogether' or 'Three children plus two children makes five children altogether'. Develop the idea of formulating a question to which the sum gives the answer. *Sophie has three apples, Peter has two apples. How many apples do they have altogether?* or *There are three children in a room. Two more come in. How many children are in the room now?*

Differentiation
Less able children may need some help with the writing of simple story problems, following the patterns of those on the photocopiable sheet.

Encourage more able children to write story problems involving larger numbers and more steps – for example: 'Three coats have 2 buttons, 5 buttons and 3 buttons. How many buttons do the coats have altogether? If each coat loses a button, how many buttons are left?'

Plenary
Let the children read their story problems to the rest of the class. Ask for solutions and explanations of methods. The answers to the questions on page 72 are: **1.** 6 pencils **2.** 8 bones **3.** 2 sweets **4.** 6 books.

Linked to
Art & design

11 Number necklaces

Objectives

Numeracy
Begin to know what each digit in a two-digit
number represents. Partition a 'teens'
number and begin to partition larger two-
digit numbers into a multiple of 10 and ones
(TU).
Art and design
Be taught about:
● visual elements including colour and
pattern
● materials and processes used in making
art, craft and design.
Links to QCA Art Unit 1B.

Resources

Threading beads (for example SUMMIT™),
strings, backing paper, pins, felt-tip pens,
copies of photocopiable page 73.

Vocabulary

units
ones
tens
teens number

Background

As children begin to read and write numbers beyond 10, they learn that the 1 in a number such as 14 represents one 'lot' or 'group' of 10. This fundamental idea must be introduced and reinforced with practical work on partitioning and exchanging sets of unit cubes and other counting objects into tens and ones. Patterns of different-coloured beads arranged on strings are a creative way of grouping and partitioning numbers. Work with such patterns can link the mathematics of grouping and partitioning to the exploration of patterns in art, design and technology. Suggest that the children look out for repeating patterns in necklaces, fabrics and other decorative items.

Preparation

Make a copy of page 74 for each child. Sort the threading beads into sets according to colour.

Main teaching activity

Demonstrate how to make repeating patterns using two different bead colours on a string. Explore how patterns can be created by grouping and repetition. Work with the children to produce a bead pattern display for the classroom. This can be assembled by pinning up strings of beads on backing paper and labelling the various patterns with the addition statements they represent. Make a range of patterns such as twos and threes (two beads of one colour alternating with three of another colour), threes and fives and so on. Ask the children to calculate the total number of beads in the basic repeating combination (for example 2 + 3 = 5) and write the corresponding sum alongside the pattern on the display.

Increase the number of beads used until you are making patterns of the type 10 + 1, 10 + 2, 10 + 3 and so on. Write down the corresponding addition statements:

$$10 + 1 = 11$$
$$10 + 2 = 12$$
$$10 + 3 = 13 \text{ etc}$$

Discuss the grouping of these patterns as tens and ones, using vocabulary such as 'one ten plus three ones equals thirteen', ' fifteen is one ten and five ones'. Indicate the bead groupings with your hands as you discuss them.

Use the photocopiable sheet to reinforce the ideas introduced in this lesson through individual work.

Differentiation

More able children could be asked to partition more than 20 beads into tens and units, and to create patterns with two, three, four and more lots of 10. Suggest that they test each other's ability to estimate quickly the number of beads on a necklace.

Less able children should concentrate on counting fewer than 20 beads on a necklace by partitioning 'teens numbers' into one ten and a number of units.

Plenary

Play a game in which you call out a number (for example, 17) and ask the children to state the number of tens and the number of units. Extend to numbers beyond 20 (for example, 53 is five tens and three units).

12 Arms, legs, fingers & toes

head   eye
ear
mouth   nose

Background

Addition and subtraction games with fingers and other body parts are an important aid to the development of number skills. Children need to practise addition and subtraction with concrete objects before they are ready to use abstract addition and subtraction facts as general number rules. As part of their work in science, children should identify the main parts of human and other animal bodies. Counting their own fingers and toes, or the legs and wings of other creatures, makes an excellent link between counting skills and work in science. You could follow this lesson with one in which mammals, reptiles, birds and minibeasts are sorted by number of legs, and simple keys are introduced. For example, a simple minibeast key might include:
0 legs? worm; 6 legs? insect ; 8 legs? spider; many legs? centipede.

Preparation

In advance of this lesson, the children should have explored basic addition and subtraction facts to 10 using unit cubes or other counting objects.

Main teaching activity

With the aid of the labelled body drawing, work with the class to compile the list shown above on the board or flip chart. Start by writing down the numbers only, then ask the children to suggest appropriate body parts to list next to each number.
Now play a game in which you ask questions such as:
● *What is the number of toes on one foot add the number of arms?*
● *What is the number of fingers take away the number of eyes?*
Use your fingers to demonstrate each addition or subtraction as you talk it through. Encourage the children to use their fingers to help them calculate by counting on or back.
Extend the range of possible questions by holding up fingers on one or two hands: *What is the number of toes take away this many fingers?*

> **A human being has:**
> 1 head, 1 nose, 1 mouth...
> 2 eyes, 2 ears, 2 arms...
> 5 fingers on one hand
> 10 toes

Differentiation

Stretch more able children by including other animal numbers, for example: *What is the number of legs on a spider take away the number of wings on a bird?*
Less able children should concentrate on simple addition and subtraction problems, using their fingers.

Plenary

Count various body parts together. The children should point to the relevant parts of their own bodies as they count: one head, one nose, one mouth, two eyes, two ears, two shoulders, two arms, two legs, five fingers, ten toes. Finally, play 'Simon Says' or sing a song related to body parts (such as 'Head, Shoulders, Knees and Toes') together.

13 Number ladder

Objectives

Numeracy
Count on and back in ones from any small number...
Understand the operations of addition and subtraction, and use the related vocabulary.
Begin to know addition facts for all pairs of numbers with a total up to at least 10, and the corresponding subtraction facts.
Literacy
Reading comprehension: read and follow simple instructions.

Resources

Copies of photocopiable page 74, card, scissors, adhesive, used matchsticks, counters (alternatively, page 74 could be photocopied onto card). An enlarged (A3) copy of page 74; a selection of board games that the children enjoy playing in class.

Vocabulary

add
more
plus
make
some
total
altogether
subtract
take away
minus
equals

Background

Simple board games such as snakes and ladders and Ludo develop number skills in an enjoyable context. Children practise addition through counting on as they throw the dice and move their counters around the board. All games have rules or instructions, and these are often displayed as a numbered list on the box or board. As children's literacy skills develop, they should become aware of this function of text and be able to follow simple rules or instructions given in the form of a list. A follow-up literacy lesson might explore some of the rules and instructions displayed around the school.

Preparation

Set out a copy of page 74 with card, glue, matchsticks, counters and scissors on each table, ready for groups to make and play the number ladder game.

Main teaching activity

Introduce the lesson with a discussion of board games and rules, using familiar examples. What is the children's favourite game? Why is it so important to follow the rules? With the children's help, write some simple numbered instructions (for example, for playing noughts and crosses) on a flip chart or OHP to use again in literacy time. Highlight the sequence of numbers for the instructions.

Emphasise that knowing and following the rules is important in making a game enjoyable and fair. Explain that the children are going to play a new number game that will help them with their addition and subtraction skills. Show the children an enlarged copy of page 74; read and discuss the instructions together. Explain that the aim is to climb the number ladder from the bottom to the top. Players take turns to spin both spinners. Adding (+) numbers takes you up the ladder. Taking away (−) numbers moves you down. If you arrive at the bottom of the ladder, you must wait there until your next turn. Set the children working in groups to make and play the game according to the instructions.

Differentiation

Challenge more able children to make their own version of the game with a longer number ladder and a greater range of numbers to add and take away. Help them to write appropriately revised, numbered instructions.
Less able children should concentrate on playing the basic game.

Plenary

Discuss the properties of the number ladder with the class. Using the enlarged version of the sheet, play the game with two counters and discuss their progress. *How many steps is the red counter ahead of the blue? Will this move take the blue ahead of the red? Where will this counter land if the instruction is take away 4?*

14 Shopping

Objectives

Numeracy
Use mental strategies to solve simple problems set in 'real life', money or measurement contexts.
Literacy
Write and draw simple instructions and labels for everyday classroom use.

Resources

Card, pens and scissors to make price tags and other shop signs; plastic or real coins. Items for 'sale', such as a selection of toys, crayons, bricks or children's artwork; copies of photocopiable page 75.

Vocabulary

money
coin
penny, pence
price
cost
buy
sell
spend
pay
change
total

Background

Shopping for sweets or other small items involves practical application of basic number skills. Adding prices, sorting coins and calculating change give practice in addition and subtraction in a real-life context. Literacy skills are also developed as the children write labels and price tags for a class shop. This shopping lesson could build on a Literacy Hour devoted to signs and labels seen in the context of shopping.

Preparation

Make a copy of page 75 for each child. Set out cards, pens and scissors on tables ready for group preparation of labels. Arrange and decorate a corner of the classroom as the class shop.

Main teaching activity

Explain that the children are going to set up a class shop and play at being shopkeepers and customers. Discuss the shopping process with the class. *How do you know how much something costs? What happens when you take your choices to the shopkeeper or till? How do you pay for your shopping? What is meant by 'change'?* Let the children choose a selection of items for sale in their shop. Discuss prices, and lead the children to set a price between 1p and 10p for each item. Make a price list on the board, then set the children to make price tags for the various items.

As a class, role-play some simple shopping transactions. Start by taking the role of shopkeeper. Distribute a selection of plastic or real coins to the children and let them purchase sets of items from you. Discuss the total price of several items, the coins that each child hands over and the change given for each transaction.

Let groups take turns to role-play shopping in the class shop area. While one group is engaged in role-play, the other children can work to answer the questions on photocopiable page 75.

Differentiation

Less able children should concentrate on purchasing a single item for up to 10p and giving the correct change.

Suggest that more able children work with prices up to 20p and make transactions in which they purchase three or more items at once. They might also like to produce 'special offer' signs, such as:

Plenary

Review the answers to page 75 with the whole class. The answers are: **1.** 5p **2.** 10p **3.** 9p **4.** 14p **5.** 12p **6.** 19p **7.** 17p **8.** 12p **9.** 10p **10.** 6p **11.** 1p. Encourage the children to continue with their shopping role-play during choosing time.

Linked to
L i t e r a c y

15 Days of the week 1

Objectives

Numeracy
Understand and use the vocabulary related to time.
Order familiar events in time.
Know the days of the week.
Literacy
Read on sight high-frequency words including days of the week.
Read and recite familiar stories and rhymes.
Use rhymes and patterned stories as models for their own writing.

Resources

A set of 'days of the week' cards for each child or pair (these can be made from photocopiable page 12); writing books and pencils; a class display of songs or poems based on the days of the week, such as 'Monday's Child' and 'Solomon Grundy' (see text on right).

Vocabulary

Monday, Tuesday...
day
week
weekend
holiday
today, yesterday, tomorrow

Background

In Year 1, as part of their work on the mathematics of time, children should learn to name the days of the week in sequence. During term time, the school week establishes a pattern in children's lives that should help them recall the sequence of the days. Each day seems to have its own character, and a discussion of children's feelings about the different days of the week could form the basis of a literacy lesson in which poems and rhymes about the sequence of the days are explored further.

Solomon Grundy
Born on Monday,
Christened on Tuesday,
Married on Wednesday,
Sick on Thursday,
Worse on Friday,
Died on Saturday,
Buried on Sunday,
That was the end
Of Solomon Grundy.

Preparation

Prepare the 'days of the week' cards and set them out on tables with notebooks and pencils. Make a large display version of the poem 'Monday's child', or an alternative poem that you have selected for display in the classroom.

Main teaching activity

Ask the children questions about the days of the week and their sequence: *What day of the week is it? How many days are there in a week? Can you name the days of the week in order? What is the first day of the school week? What is the last day of the school week? How many days are there in the school week? How many days are there at the weekend? What are the weekend days called?*

Hold up the day name cards in turn and ask the children to describe something special that happens on each day. For example, Monday is PE apparatus day, Tuesday is class assembly day, and so on. Ask: *Which is your favourite school day? Which is your favourite weekend day? Why?*

Monday's child is fair of face,
Tuesday's child is full of grace,
Wednesday's child is full of woe,
Thursday's child has far to go,
Friday's child is loving and giving,
Saturday's child works hard for a living,
But the child that is born on the Sabbath day
Is bonny and blithe and good and gay.

The children should now work on their own or in pairs with a set of day name cards. Ask them to put the cards into the right order and then write a short sentence about each day. This writing could take the form of a poem or rhyme:

> **Monday back to school,**
> **Tuesday swimming pool,**
> **Wednesday have PE,**
> **Thursday chips for tea,**
> **Friday stay up late,**
> **Saturday roller-skate,**
> **Sunday watch TV,**
> **Monday back to school...**

Differentiation

Less able children should concentrate on ordering, remembering and writing out the names of the days of the week.

Encourage more able children to write poems and rhymes using the day names.

Plenary

Read out some of the children's poetry. Read and discuss the poem 'Monday's Child' as a class. Ask: *Does the day on which you are born really affect what you are like, or is it just a nice poem?* As a class, try to compose an alternative 'Monday's Child' poem. As a homework activity, ask the children to find out which day of the week they were born on.

Linked to
S c i e n c e
M u s i c

16 Musical instruments

Background

Classifying and sorting are important skills, not only in mathematics but in science and other areas of the curriculum. There are numerous opportunities in the school day for identifying the characteristics by which objects or events can be classified and sorted into sets. For example, toys can be sorted as soft or hard, with wheels or without wheels, indoor or outdoor. Living things can be classified as animals or plants, days as school days or holidays, and so on. In science, children should learn that sound sources produce sounds in different ways. In music, they should begin to recognise the different classes of musical instruments: percussion, wind and string. A sorting exercise in which the school instruments are grouped in sets according to how they produce sound forms the basis of a numeracy lesson that links to both science and music.

Preparation

Distribute the musical instruments at random between boxes. Make sure that there are examples of each of the three categories of instrument in each box.

Main teaching activity

Introduce the lesson to the class by discussing and demonstrating how different instruments are played to produce sounds. Percussion instruments are tapped, rattled or banged. Wind instruments are blown. Stringed instruments are plucked or bowed. Pick up each instrument in turn and discuss its characteristics.

Ask the children to work in groups with boxes of instruments, sorting each collection into three sets. They should use cards to label each set and make a list of the

Objectives

Numeracy
Solve a given problem by sorting, classifying and organising information in simple ways, such as: using objects or pictures; in a list or simple table.

Science
Be taught that there are many kinds of sound and sources of sound.

Music
Be taught how sounds can be made in different ways.

Links to QCA Science Unit 1F and Music Unit 2.

Resources

Boxes containing various musical instruments for sorting; cards, pencils; large sheets of paper, coloured pencils or crayons; a poster or photograph of an orchestra.

Vocabulary

count
sort
set
group
list

instruments in it. Then they should make posters to illustrate examples of the three different types of instrument. The posters should be labelled 'Wind', 'Strings' and 'Percussion'. The children can draw pictures of various instruments being played, perhaps using the poster of an orchestra for reference.

list of instruments with ones they have seen or played elsewhere. Discuss how the sets can be subdivided – for example, wind instruments are usually classified as either woodwind or brass, depending on which material they used to be made from.

Plenary

Display the children's posters and ask the class to identify the instruments shown. Look at a poster or photograph of an orchestra and identify the types of instrument being played in the different sections.

Differentiation

Less able children should concentrate on categorising the instruments available in the classroom.

Ask more able children to extend their

17 Assessment 1

Objectives

The assessment activities in this book are designed to introduce Key Stage 1 children to SAT-style questions. They are set in cross-curricular contexts based on the preceding term's lessons. The questions in Assessment 1 test the children's progress in: sequencing odd and even numbers; working with money; sorting and classifying.

Resources

Copies of photocopiable page 76, pencils. A pack of number cards to 20.

Preparation

Make one copy per child of page 76. If you feel that this sheet is too 'busy', the three activities could be separated and enlarged on individual sheets.

Introduction

Review how the relevant cross-curricular topics have been covered during the term. Remind the children of some of the projects and investigations they have undertaken, and ask them to recall and recount their work. Emphasise the mathematical content – for example, *Do you remember how the odd-numbered houses were on one side of the street and the even-numbered houses were on the other side?*

Main assessment activity

Give each child a copy of page 76 to work on individually. Guide the whole class through the questions one at a time, reading

the text with them and prompting them to work out and write down their answers. Try to make the whole activity enjoyable!

Practical activity

Shuffle a set of number cards to 10. Ask the child to sequence these cards in a line. Can he or she say the correct number name while pointing at each card? Repeat with number cards to 20. Select two single-digit cards and ask the child to add the numbers. Now ask him or her to take the smaller number from the larger one.

Plenary

Review the answers as a class. Collect the completed assessment sheets to use as an aid to judging individual children's progress, and your records. The answers are:

1 3 5 7 9 11 13 15
2 4 6 8 10 12 14 16

Sophie has 8p, Sunita has 20p.

Strings – violin, guitar, banjo.
Wind – recorder, flute, trumpet.
Percussion – drum, cymbal, triangle.

18 Number songs & rhymes

Objectives

Numeracy
Know the number names and recite them in order to at least 20, from and back to zero.
Count on in twos from zero, then one, and begin to recognise odd and even numbers.
Literacy
Learn and recite simple poems and rhymes, with actions, and re-read them from the text.
Music
Use their voices expressively by singing songs and speaking chants and rhymes.
Links to QCA Music Unit 1.

Resources

A selection of number songs and rhymes for the class to learn (see 'Background' for examples); objects or illustrations to accompany these, such as ten green plastic lemonade bottles; a number chart; paper, pencils; coloured pencils or crayons.

Vocabulary

number
zero, one, two, three... twenty (and beyond)
count on
count back
count in twos
every other
pattern
even
odd

Background

Number songs and rhymes develop counting skills through repetition and association of numbers with familiar objects and events. Learning and chanting songs and rhymes with repetitive structures based on number sequences links children's developing mathematical knowledge to their work in literacy and music. A selection of number songs and rhymes for the class to learn could include: 'Ten green bottles'; 'One, two, buckle my shoe'; 'One, two, three, four, five, once I caught a fish alive'; 'There were ten in the bed'; 'The animals went in two by two'; 'Two, four, six, eight, Mary at the garden gate'; 'The twelve days of Christmas'; 'Green grow the rushes, oh'.
    Follow-up lessons could include the creation of classroom displays based on favourite number songs and rhymes.

Preparation

Make a display of one or more of the verses or rhymes in advance of the lesson. Place the objects you have selected to illustrate the rhyme (for example, ten green plastic bottles) and the number chart so that they can be seen by all the children.

Main teaching activity

Teach the rhymes to the whole class, singing or chanting the verses together. Choose individual children to point to objects and/or the number chart as you reach the appropriate points in the rhymes. The children can make their own illustrations for the chosen songs to be displayed on the classroom wall.

Differentiation

All the children should be able to learn simple rhymes such as 'One, two, buckle my shoe' and 'Two, four, six, eight, Mary at the garden gate'.
    Encourage more able children to learn more complex rhymes such as 'There were ten in the bed' and 'The twelve days of Christmas', which involve counting backwards.

Plenary

Conclude the lesson with some whole-class counting practice forwards to, and backwards from, 10, 12 and 20. The newly-learned number songs and rhymes should be chanted at frequent intervals during the school week. For example, you could choose a different number rhyme or song as a warm-up to introduce the numeracy lesson each day.

19 Dot-to-dot

Objectives

Numeracy
Read and write numerals from zero to at least 20.
Order numbers to at least 20, and position them on a number track.
ICT
Be taught how to plan and give instructions to make things happen.
Be taught to present their completed work effectively.
Explore a variety of ICT tools.
Links to QCA IT Unit 1A.

Resources

A large dot-to-dot picture drawn on the board or a sheet of paper; copies of photocopiable page 77; a computer system set up with *Textease, Microsoft Word* or a similar word-processing and drawing program.

Vocabulary

zero, one, two, three... twenty (and beyond)
order
next
count
draw a line between
join

Background

To complete a dot-to-dot picture, children need to read and sequence numerals. Completing such pictures is an enjoyable way of developing counting and sequencing skills. Dot-to-dot pictures can be created easily on a computer screen using programs such as *Textease* (Softease Ltd), *Word* (Microsoft) or *Publisher* (GreenStreet Technology). Completing the picture involves development of mouse skills and use of the computer to create and print a drawing-based document.

Preparation

Make a copy of page 77 for each child.

Prepare a demonstration on screen by creating 20 numbered points that can be dragged around the page to make a dot-to-dot picture or pattern. In *Textease*, this is achieved simply by entering a full stop followed by a numeral at 20 arbitrary locations on the page. A sample screen is shown below. Details of *Textease* are available from www.textease.com.

Main teaching activity

Introduce the lesson by completing the demonstration dot-to-dot picture with the whole class. Ask the children to tell you where to move next as you use your pen or chalk to connect the points. Now ask the children to

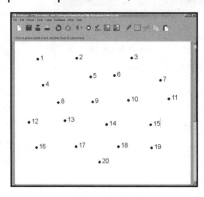

complete the dot-to-dot picture on the photocopiable sheet, and then to create their own dot-to-dot puzzles on the computer screen. Show them how to drag the numbered dots around the screen to create their design. When they have completed their puzzles, the children can print them for their friends to complete.

Details of *Textease* are available from www.textease.com

Differentiation

Less able children could create puzzles using numbers to 10.

More able children could extend their dot-to-dot puzzles beyond 20.

Plenary

Discuss the children's puzzles as a class. Ask the children to use a finger to trace their designs on paper from dot to dot, saying the numbers as they do so. Display the children's work in the classroom.

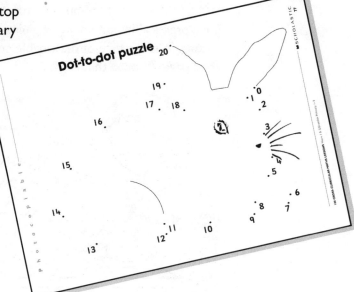

Linked to
D & T

20 Home-made dice

Objectives

Numeracy
Begin to know addition facts for all pairs of numbers with a total up to at least 10, and the corresponding subtraction facts.
Use everyday language to describe features of familiar 3-D shapes.
Make and describe models.
Begin to relate solid shapes to pictures of them.

Design and technology
Measure, mark out, cut and shape a range of materials.
Assemble, join and combine materials and components.
Links to QCA Design and technology Units 1A, 1B and 1D.

Resources
Copies of photocopiable page 78 on thin card, scissors, adhesive, felt-tip pens, building bricks (optional), thin card squares (optional); a large demonstration dice.

Vocabulary
dice
cube
face
add
sum
total
score
subtract
take away
minus
leave

Background
All children at Year 1 should be familiar with conventional cubic gaming dice from various board games. Dice are extremely useful in mathematics lessons for generating small random numbers to turn addition and subtraction practice into an enjoyable game. In this lesson, the children make their own dice and label them with numbers appropriate to their addition and subtraction skills. Making a dice develops the technology skills of cutting, shaping, assembling and joining, which the children will use in other practical lessons.

Preparation
Set out the materials on tables, according to your normal practice for a practical lesson involving gluing and cutting. To make dice of reasonable strength, copy page 78 onto thin card.

Main teaching activity
Discuss the properties of the demonstration dice with the whole class. *What shape is it?* (A cube.) *How many faces does it have?* (Six.) *How are the faces numbered?* (1, 2, 3, 4, 5, 6.) If the numbers are displayed as dots, discuss the patterns used to make the numbers easy to recognise. *If you add the numbers on opposite faces, what answers do you get?* (Always 7.)

Explain that the children are going to make their own dice to play a number game. Show them the photocopiable sheet and explain how to cut out the dice net, number it (using numerals rather than dots) and then fold and stick it to make a cube. Some children may need adult help to cut, fold and stick accurately. (Alternatively, less dextrous children could cut out card squares, number them and tape them to a cubic building brick.) Let the children choose their own numbers to label their dice. The numbers do not need to be 1–6 as on a conventional dice. Suggest that some children select numbers in the range 0–5, while others choose numbers at random up to 10.

Show the children how to play simple games with their numbered dice. Throw two dice. *What is the sum of the two numbers? What answer do you get when you take the smaller number away from the bigger number?*

Differentiation
Less able children should play games with pairs of dice, each numbered up to 5. This will enable them to practise addition and subtraction of numbers to 10. More able children could use dice numbered up to 10 to practise addition and subtraction of numbers to 20.

Plenary
Use two dice to generate numbers for the children to add and subtract. Spend several minutes on mental calculations with the whole class to reinforce addition and subtraction facts – first to 10, then to 20.

21 How many minibeasts?

Objectives

Numeracy
Understand and use the vocabulary of estimation.
Give a sensible estimate of a number of objects that can be checked by counting (for example up to about 30 objects).
Science
Group living things according to observable similarities and differences.

Resources

A box of small plastic minibeasts for sorting and counting (see illustration), a large piece of thick card.

Vocabulary

guess how many
estimate
nearly
roughly
close to
about the same as
just over
just under
too many
too few

Background

Most children will be able to recognise a group of up to five or six objects, but they are unlikely to make a sensible estimate of larger numbers without considerable practice and discussion of estimation methods. To estimate the number in a group of around 10 objects, we need to see the group as being about twice as big as a group of five. A set that is twice as big again must contain about 20 objects. These estimation skills can be developed with any similar counting objects, such as unit cubes, beads or plastic animals. In this lesson, the children identify, group and estimate numbers of plastic minibeasts, linking to work in science on the classification of living things. The lesson will reinforce the knowledge that insects have six legs, spiders eight legs, centipedes many legs, slugs no legs, and so on.

Preparation

This lesson could follow on from a science lesson in which the characteristics of different minibeasts have been studied.

Main teaching activity

Count a few small sets of plastic minibeasts (up to 10) together. Now tell the children that you want them to 'estimate' the number in a set without counting. Explain that an estimate is a 'sensible guess'. An estimate can be checked by counting, and a good estimate will be quite close to the actual number.
Arrange a set of five minibeasts behind a piece of card. Remove the card and ask the

children to call out the number they think are there without counting them one by one. Count to check their estimates. Repeat the exercise with various numbers of minibeasts up to 20, and then up to 30. Discuss strategies for making a good estimate – for example, spotting a sub-group of five and then judging how much bigger the whole group is.

Extend the activity by asking the children to pick out different types of minibeasts in their estimates. For example, show a mixture of about 20 minibeasts and ask for rapid responses to questions such as *How many insects? How many spiders? How many worms?* You could also ask for estimates such as the total number of legs or antennae. Count to check.

Differentiation

Less able children should make estimates using numbers up to 10.
Challenge more able children to estimate numbers up to 30.

Plenary

Conclude with a discussion to reinforce the meaning of the word **estimate**. Give examples of good and poor estimates – for example, 30 might be a good estimate of the number of children in the class, but 10 or 60 would be a poor estimate.

Linked to
Geography
Science

22 Postage stamps

Objectives

Numeracy
Use mental strategies to solve simple problems set in 'real life', money or measurement contexts.
Find totals and change from up to 20p.
Measure using uniform non-standard units.

Geography
Make observations about where things are located.
Study the locality of the school.

Science
Make and record measurements.
Links to QCA Geography Unit 1.

Resources

Sheets of plain sticky labels, felt-tip pens; a classroom balancing scales; wooden bricks or similar uniform objects; a few sheets of real stamps (using low denominations such as 2p, 5p and 10p); plastic coins.

Vocabulary

cost
weight
balance
money
penny, pence
costs more, costs less
how much?
how many?
buy
price

Background

Children find decorative stickers and stamps appealing to look at and use. Sheets of stickers and stamps provide opportunities for mathematical discussion and activities. Stamps can be purchased in a sheet: a regular array that can be counted in groups. The stamps are labelled with their value, which can be matched to the values of coins. The cost of a sheet of 2p stamps can be calculated by counting in twos. The value of the stamps needed to post an item depends on its mass. Children in Year 1 are not ready to use the actual Post Office price charts, but could work with a simplified system for sending different-sized packages around the school. Work on stamps and postage links to geography lessons in which children study their school and local environment. Weighing letters and parcels also links to measurement skills in science.

Preparation

Set out the sticky labels and pens on the tables. Set up the balancing scales where the children can use them as they work in groups.

Main teaching activity

Discuss posting letters and purchasing stamps with the class. *Where is the local Post Office? How much does it cost to send a postcard or a birthday card? What is the*

difference between first-class and second-class post? Why are parcels weighed at the Post Office? Show the children some sheets of stamps and use them for counting up prices. *How many stamps are there on a sheet? What is the value of each stamp? How much does the whole sheet cost?*

Ask the children to make their own stamps for sending letters and parcels around the school. Show them the sheets of labels and discuss the designs and values of the stamps they will produce. For example, they might decide that the cost of sending a letter or card is 5p within the class and 10p to another class. Parcel costs could be mass-related, and a simple scale could be established using a balance.

Different-sized wooden bricks or similar objects could be used to set the mass limits. The children should design and make stamps, role-play post office transactions, and deliver letters and parcels around the school.

Differentiation

Less able children could concentrate on producing a sheet of 'letter' stamps of the same value, for example 5p. Can they count their stamps? Can they find the total value of the stamps on the sheet by counting in fives?

More able children could develop a wider range of stamp values and relate them to letter and parcel masses.

Plenary

Use the stamps the children have made for some counting and calculation exercises.

Linked to
Literacy

23 Addition words

Objectives

Numeracy
Understand the operation of addition and use the related vocabulary.
Begin to use the +, − and = signs to record mental calculations in a number sentence.

Literacy
Make collections of significant words and words linked to particular topics.

Resources

A set of numeral cards, number word cards (photocopiable pages 8–11) and mathematical symbol and vocabulary cards (photocopiable page 79); copies of photocopiable page 80, pencils.

Vocabulary

add
plus
more
make
some
total
altogether
equal

Background

Simple mathematical problems can be expressed in a variety of ways, using a number of equivalent words. The words *sum, total, add, plus* and *altogether* can all be used to express the idea of addition. Children's mathematical vocabulary should be developed by expressing oral problems in a variety of ways, and rephrasing them in alternative words. In Year 1, children should also begin to read 'number 'sentences' written in symbols – for example, reading 3 + 5 = 8 as 'three plus five equals eight'.

In this lesson, the children translate and match addition problems expressed in various ways, using words, figures and symbols. The lesson is linked to word-level vocabulary work in literacy, since the children are making a collection of words linked to the topic of addition.

Preparation

Prepare the sets of cards from page 79 for demonstration. Make one copy per child of page 80.

Main teaching activity

Flash the mathematical vocabulary and symbol cards to check that the children can read these words and symbols in isolation. Use these cards together with number name and numeral cards to create some equivalent mathematical statements, such as:

> 3 + 4 = 7
> three add four makes seven
> the sum of three and four is seven
> 3 plus 4 equals 7
> three plus four totals seven

Choose another sum and ask individual children to restate it in different ways. Ask the children to work in pairs to complete the exercise on page 80 by matching the pairs of equivalent statements on the sheet.

Differentiation

Less able children should concentrate on the matching activity on page 80. Check that they can read all the vocabulary.

Challenge more able children to write further alternative expressions for each of the statements on the sheet.

Plenary

Conclude the lesson with some quick-fire addition practice to 10. Express the addition problems in a variety of ways, such as:
● *Add 3 to 4.*
● *What is the total of 4 and 6?*
● *3 plus 2*
● *What must I add to 4 to make 7?*
● *4 plus 2 equals...*
● *If I have 5 and 3 more, how many do I have altogether?*

Linked to
Science

24 Compare and order

Objectives

Numeracy
Compare two lengths by direct comparison; extend to more than two.
Science
Make simple comparisons and identify simple patterns or associations.

Resources

Trays with collections of different-sized natural items – for example, trays of pebbles, conkers, leaves and fir cones.

Vocabulary

order
compare
longer
shorter
taller
bigger
smaller
longest
shortest

Background
The basis of measurement is a comparison between the item to be measured and the standard units on a scale or balance. Making direct comparisons between the lengths of a variety of objects prepares children for the measurement process. Objects such as pebbles, conkers, leaves and fir cones can be compared and sorted according to size. Making comparisons based on careful observation is an important component of many science activities.

Developing strategies for sorting and sequencing items according to given characteristics also links with work in ICT.

Preparation
Set out the trays of objects on tables in preparation for group work.

Main teaching activity
Introduce the lesson by ordering the children according to height. Ask two children to stand back to back so that the rest of the class can make a comparison. Compare a third child with the first pair. Place him or her to the right, to the left or in the centre, so that the three are arranged in order of height. Add a fourth child to the row, making appropriate height comparisons to position him or her correctly. Continue to sort all the children in the class. Use the appropriate vocabulary of comparison: *taller than, not as tall as* and so on.

Ask the children to work in groups to compare and order the items in the trays by size, using the strategy you have demonstrated with the children's heights: they should take the items one at a time and make side-by-side comparisons to position each item correctly in the sequence.

Differentiation
Less able children can concentrate on ordering items by length. More able children could develop the procedure to sort items by mass (for example, irregular pebbles) by using a balance to make comparisons between pairs of objects.

Plenary
Conclude the lesson with some questions on the ordered sets to develop the children's vocabulary of comparison. *Which is the shorter/longer of these two leaves? Which is the shortest/longest fir cone in the set?*

25 Shape patterns

Objectives

Numeracy
Use one or more shapes to make, continue and describe repeating patterns.

Art and design
Be taught about visual elements, including pattern and shape.

Resources

Trays of plastic shapes for children to create their own repeating patterns; copies of photocopiable page 81.

Vocabulary

shape
pattern
repeat
triangle
rectangle
square
circle
oval

Background

In this lesson, the children use shape names to describe repeating patterns created from two-dimensional shapes. They begin to recognise the characteristic features of basic shapes such as triangles, rectangles, squares, circles and ovals, and to see how a pattern is created through repetition of one or more basic units. This lesson can be linked to lessons on shape and pattern in art, design and technology.

Preparation

Make one copy of page 81 for each child. Set out trays of plastic shapes on tables.

Main teaching activity

Introduce the lesson by selecting plastic shapes from a tray and asking the children to name and describe them. The key ideas to highlight are: a triangle has three straight sides; a rectangle has four straight sides and 'square' corners; a square has four equal sides and 'square' corners; a circle has a smooth curved edge like a wheel, and looks the same whichever way you turn it; an oval looks like a stretched circle. Create a repeating pattern with the shapes, such as the example shown below.

Ask the children to describe this pattern using the shape names. *What sequence of shapes is repeated to make this pattern?* Say together:

> **square, circle, triangle, square, circle, triangle…**

Set out one or two more examples to describe as a class. Ask the children to work on the photocopiable sheet, investigating and describing the various shape patterns. Suggest that they colour the shapes to show the basic repeating group. For example, they could colour the first group of shapes red and the second group blue, then repeat, alternating the two colours for successive groups.

Differentiation

Less able children could use plastic shapes to match the patterns on the photocopiable worksheet.

Suggest that more able children create their own more complex repeating patterns based on a group of four, five or more shapes. They might set out the patterns with plastic shapes initially, then draw and describe them in their workbooks.

Plenary

Review the photocopiable sheet with the whole class. The answers are: triangle, rectangle (on its side); star, circle, triangle; circle, rectangle (on end), triangle, square; square, oval (on its side), diamond, hexagon. Look at some of the shape patterns that the children have created for themselves. As a class, check to confirm that the pattern is repeated regularly.

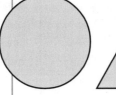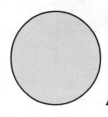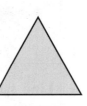

Linked to

26 Fold in half

Objectives

Numeracy
Make and describe patterns and pictures.
Fold shapes in half, then make them into
symmetrical patterns.
Art and design
Be taught about visual elements, including
pattern and shape.
Links to QCA Art Unit 1: A Self-portrait.

Resources

A copy of photocopiable page 82 for each
child; scissors, coloured felt-tip pens; large
versions of basic shapes (square, rectangle,
isosceles triangle, irregular triangle,
parallelogram) cut from paper for
demonstration.

Vocabulary

symmetrical
match
shape
half
fold
circle
triangle
square
rectangle
star

Background

Symmetrical shapes such as squares, rectangles, isosceles triangles, circles and stars can be folded in half in such a way that one half of the shape exactly covers the other. A shape with this property has one or more lines that divide it into parts that are mirror images of each other. In this activity, the children investigate the effect of folding simple shapes cut from paper. They describe a shape that can be folded in half as 'symmetrical' and a shape that cannot be folded in this way as 'not symmetrical'. In doing this, they are developing their artistic awareness of pattern and shape. Follow-up work in art, design and technology might involve the children making symmetrical designs for greetings cards or calendars.

Preparation

Set out copies of page 82, scissors and felt-tip pens on tables before the lesson.

Main teaching activity

Introduce the lesson by showing the children examples of paper shapes (square, rectangle, isosceles triangle, irregular triangle, parallelogram) and asking them which shapes can be folded in half. Demonstrate that only certain shapes can be folded into matching halves. Introduce the words *symmetrical* and *non-symmetrical* to classify the different shapes. Ask the children to cut out the shapes from the photocopiable sheet and find out which of them are symmetrical. Suggest that they colour matching halves differently. They can also use scissors to cut out small pieces of the folded shapes in order to create other types of symmetrical pattern.

Differentiation

Less able children should concentrate on sorting shapes that can be folded into matching halves from those that cannot. Most children should discover that there is more than one way of folding a square or a rectangle into matching halves.

Challenge more able children to investigate whether it is possible to fold their shapes further (for example, a rectangle can be folded into quarters).

Plenary

Review the children's findings with the whole class. Use their cut-out and coloured shapes to create a wall display. Ask the children: *What else is symmetrical?* Point out that their faces are almost, but not quite, symmetrical.

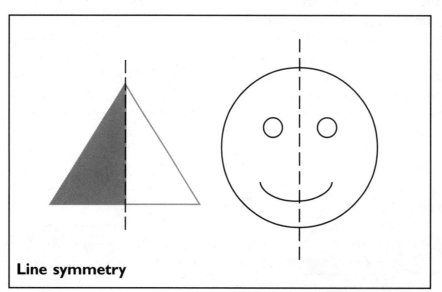

Line symmetry

27 Number track

| 20 |
| 19 |
| 18 |
| 17 |
| 16 |
| 15 |
| 14 |
| 13 |
| 12 |
| 11 |
| 10 |
| 9 |
| 8 |
| 7 |
| 6 |
| 5 |
| 4 |
| 3 |
| 2 |
| 1 |
| 0 |

Objectives

Numeracy
Describe and extend number sequences: count on and back in ones from any small number; count on in twos from zero, then 1, and begin to recognise odd or even numbers to about 20 as 'every other number'; count in steps of 5 from zero to 20 or more, then back again; begin to count on in steps of 3 from zero.

PE
Perform basic skills in travelling and being still, both on the floor and using apparatus. **Links to QCA PE Gymnastic activities Unit 1.**

Resources

Chalk, a playground; balls, beanbags, hoops and other equipment for simple games (optional).

Vocabulary

number track
count
count on
count back
count in ones, twos... fives...
odd, even
every other

Background

The traditional playground game of hopscotch develops both physical and counting skills. In this activity, it is adapted to practise counting in steps of 1, 2, 3 and 5 from 0 to 20 and back again in the context of PE activities. In this way, the children develop both their counting skills and their control of rapid movement.

Preparation

Chalk four large number tracks on the playground and label them with the numbers 0–20 (see illustration). The squares should be a suitable size so that the children can hop, jump or step between them (that is, approximately 30cm × 30cm). Prepare for a PE lesson according to your normal practice.

Main teaching activity

Show the children the number tracks in the playground. If you prefer, you could leave the squares blank and then number them with the children, counting from 0 to 20 together as you do so. Divide the children into four groups and line up each group at the start (0) of one of the tracks. Play a variety of counting games in which the children take turns, following one after another, to step, hop or jump from square to square,

counting as they do so. Possible games include: step on every square; step on the odd numbers; hop on the even numbers; step 3 at a time; step or hop 5 at a time; step or hop back towards zero in various intervals.

You could also use the number tracks as scoreboards, with a human marker who moves along each track as a team scores points in simple skill games. These games could include throwing beanbags into numbered hoops, throwing and catching a ball a set number of times, and so on.

Differentiation

Less able groups should concentrate on counting up along the number track in steps of 1 and 2.

Challenge more able groups to devise their own games using the number tracks, in which they start from different points and count on or back in steps of 1, 2 or 5.

Plenary

Conclude the lesson with some whole-class counting (on and back) in ones, twos and fives. Start at different points on the track and use human markers to move along the track or raise their hands as you count.

28 What's the time, Mr Wolf?

Objectives

Numeracy
Read the time to the hour or half-hour on analogue clocks.
Literacy
Learn and recite simple poems and rhymes.

Resources

A large analogue clock face for demonstration; books or posters with poems, stories, songs and rhymes about time (see Background).

Vocabulary

clock
o'clock
hands
big hand
little hand
hour
minute
half past
dinner time

Background

In Year 1, children should be introduced to the analogue clock face and read time to the nearest hour and half-hour. The game 'What's the time, Mr Wolf?' provides an excellent opportunity to build on initial work on time. Clocks and time feature in a number of songs, poems and stories that can be used to link work in literacy to work on time in mathematics. Examples include 'Hickory, Dickory, Dock', 'My Grandfather's Clock' (in *Tinder-Box Assembly Book* edited by Sylvia Barrett, A&C Black) and 'Cinderella'.

Preparation

Set the clock face up where the whole class can see it.

Main teaching activity

Introduce the lesson with the analogue clock face, turning the hands and counting through the hours: *one o'clock, two o'clock, three o'clock...* Link the times on the clock to times in popular stories, songs and rhymes. Read out or recite your selection of time stories, poems and songs. Ask questions such as: *What was the time when the mouse ran up the clock? When did Cinderella have to return from the ball?* Proceed to demonstrate how the

hands are positioned on the half-hours and count them through: *half past one, half past two, half past three...*

Follow up by playing the game 'What's the time, Mr Wolf?' This is probably best played in the school hall or another large space. You could modify the game as follows. Choose one child to be Mr Wolf, who turns his or her back on the other children. You set a time on the clock face. The children chant: 'What's the time, Mr Wolf?' Mr Wolf replies with the time on the clock face, and the children step forward silently by the appropriate number of steps. The chant is repeated and Mr Wolf gives the new time. When it is 12 o'clock he or she says 'Dinner time!', then turns around and chases the children, who must escape to the walls. The first person caught becomes the new Mr Wolf.

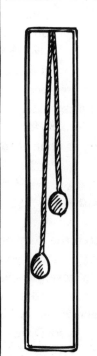

Differentiation

Differentiate by setting times according to Mr Wolf's ability to read the clock.

Plenary

Conclude the lesson by asking for volunteers to come to the front to demonstrate various specified times on the clock face.

29 Dominoes

Objectives

Numeracy
Solve simple mathematical problems or puzzles; recognise and predict from simple patterns and relationships.
History
Ask questions about the past.
Study changes in the way of life of their family or others around them.
Links to QCA History Unit 1.

Resources

A set of dominoes for each pair of children (see Preparation); a set of wooden dominoes for demonstration.

Vocabulary

domino
total
sequence
double

Background

Many popular parlour games such as Bingo, Ludo and dominoes develop counting, sequencing and addition skills. Work in mathematics lessons based on these games links to work in history on games that children used to play.

Preparation

The children could bring dominoes from home, and the different sets could be displayed in the classroom. Alternatively, the children could make paper (or card) dominoes from copies of photocopiable page 83. Set out dominoes (or copies of page 83) and scissors on tables before the lesson.

Main teaching activity

Discuss the game of dominoes. Ask the children: *Do you play dominoes at home? Who taught you – your parents? Your grandparents? Who did they learn the game from?* Suggest that the children ask their parents or grandparents about their memories of playing dominoes when they were young. *What did the dominoes look like?*

Demonstrate a simple version of the game using a set of wooden dominoes. Show how the dominoes are divided between the players. Players take turns to try to put down a domino. You can only put down a domino if you can match the number to a free end of the dominoes already laid. A number can also be matched to a double by placing it against the mid-point of the domino (see illustration). The first person to put down all his or her dominoes wins. Let the children play a game of dominoes in pairs or small groups.

Set the class some simple investigations to carry out with their sets of dominoes.
● *How many spots are there on each domino?*
● *Can you place them in sequence according to the number of spots?*
● *Can you predict the smallest number of spots on a domino? What about the largest number? Count to check.*
● *Which dominoes have an even number of spots? Which have an odd number?*

Differentiation

Less able children should concentrate on counting the spots on individual dominoes.

Challenge more able children with some domino-based calculations – for example: *Find two dominoes with a total of 11 spots.*

Plenary

Review the results of the children's investigations as a class. In front of the class, sort a set of dominoes into sub-sets with equal numbers of dots. Use this exercise to discuss number bonds such as:
5 + 1 = 4 + 2 = 3 + 3

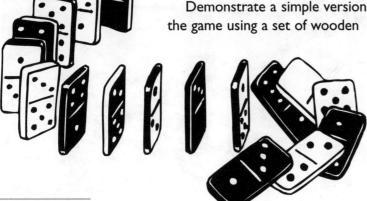

30 Postcard puzzles

Objectives

Numeracy
Solve simple mathematical problems or puzzles; recognise and predict from simple patterns and relationships.
Geography
Identify and describe what places are like.
Identify and describe where places are.
Recognise how places compare with other places.
Links to QCA Geography Unit 1.

Resources

A selection of local postcards or photographs (one per child) that can be cut up to make puzzles; two large postcards showing different scenes; scissors.

Vocabulary

puzzle
shape
piece
assemble
put together

Background

Solving simple shape puzzles and jigsaws develops knowledge of shape and spatial relationships (see also Lesson 8, 'Tangrams'). Two or three straight cuts at different angles made with a pair of scissors divide a rectangular postcard or photograph into triangles and quadrilaterals, making a puzzle for children to put back together. Puzzles made in this way from local postcards and photographs can be linked to work in geography looking at the local environment.

Preparation

Set out the cards and scissors on tables in preparation for the lesson. Cut up a pair of large postcards to make a puzzle for the whole class to solve.

Main teaching activity

Introduce the lesson by showing the class the jumbled pieces of the two cards. Explain that you 'accidentally' cut them up when you were doing some cutting-out for the classroom. You need to put them back together in order to find out where they are from. Assemble the two cards with the help of the whole class. Discuss the features that enable them to identify part of a card as showing a particular location. Look in particular for features such as the sea or sand to identify the coast, woods or mountains indicating countryside, or lots of buildings and busy streets suggesting a city.

Explain that the children are going to make their own postcard puzzles. Ask them to work in pairs, cutting a card each and shuffling the pieces. Pairs should then swap puzzles and try to reassemble the cards.

Differentiation

Challenge more able children to cut their cards into five or more pieces.

Less able children should cut their cards into no more than three pieces.

Plenary

Make a display of the reassembled cards. Discuss the shapes of various pieces, and conclude the lesson by identifying the locations shown on the cards.

31 Giving change

Objectives

Numeracy
Recognise coins of different values.
Solve simple problems set in 'real life' or
money contexts.
Geography
Make observations about where things
are located.
Links to QCA Geography Unit 1.

Resources

Plastic 1p, 2p, 5p, 10p and 20p coins; paper
and pencils; a set of real coins to show
the class.

Vocabulary

money
penny, pence
coin
change
equal

Background

In Year 1, children should be able to exchange a 20p piece for an equivalent value in smaller coins. This process develops their knowledge of addition facts to 20. In this lesson, the children's ability to calculate and give change is linked to their awareness of local shops, amusements and facilities in geography. Children or their parents may have needed change to purchase items from slot machines, feed parking meters or use public telephones.

Preparation

Set out plastic coins, paper and pencils on tables in preparation for group work.

Main teaching activity

Introduce the lesson by discussing the process of paying and receiving change. Can the children think of any situations in which they need to change larger-value coins into smaller-value ones? For example, they might do this to make a purchase from a vending machine, to use a public telephone, or to ride on a machine in an amusement arcade or shopping centre. Discuss why we use these machines. For example: vending machines are available even when the shops are closed; ticket machines allow a company to employ fewer ticket sellers, and help to reduce queues at the ticket office.

With the class, role-play going to a counter to change 10p and 20p coins into smaller coins. Make sure the children understand that for the exchange to be fair, the total value of the smaller coins given as change must be equal to the value of the

larger coin. Set the children to work in groups to investigate how many different ways there are of making up 2p, 5p, 10p and 20p. They should list the possibilities as follows:

10p = 5p + 5p
10p = 5p + 2p + 2p + 1p
10p = 5p + 2p + 1p + 1p + 1p
and so on.

Differentiation

Less able groups should concentrate on giving change up to 10p.

Challenge more able groups to investigate changing 20p into smaller-value coins. Do not expect them to find all the possible ways of making up 10p and 20p at this stage: they are not ready to list all the possible combinations systematically.

Plenary

Ask representatives of the groups to describe their findings. How many different ways did they find to make up the different amounts? Were the methods used by the different groups the same, or did they differ? Check some of the transactions with actual coins. Finally, ask the children to list as many locations of coin-operated machines as they can in the locality.

32 Fill your basket

Objectives

Numeracy
Recognise coins of different values.
Solve simple problems set in 'real life' or money contexts.
Design and technology
Carry out design and make assignments using a range of materials.
Links to QCA Design and Technology Unit 1C: Eat more fruit and vegetables.

Resources

A copy of photocopiable page 84 for each group, scissors; plastic trays or other containers to serve as 'baskets', plastic coins.

Vocabulary

buy
spend
price
money
coin
pence
total

Background

This lesson builds on the previous lesson ('Giving change') to develop addition skills to 20 in the context of transactions involving money. The children fill their baskets with fruit and vegetables cut from a photocopiable sheet. The game could be made more realistic by asking the children to make model fruit and vegetables from modelling clay or papier mâché for purchase from a class fruit stall. Making, recognising and naming the various fruit and vegetables links to work in technology, art and science.

should work together to select items, calculating their total spending as they do so, and fill their basket to the value specified. Review their progress periodically, comparing the selections made by different groups to fill their baskets to a given total. For example, one group might select four oranges at 5p each to fill their basket for 20p, whereas another group might select a potato, an apple, a pear, a banana and a grapefruit: 1p + 2p + 2p + 5p + 10p = 20p.

Differentiation

Less able children should fill their baskets to the value of 10p or 20p.

Challenge groups of more able children to fill their baskets to higher totals, such as 25p or 50p.

Plenary

Review the selections made by different groups. Can the children suggest any other combinations to make the specified totals? Discuss the advantages of buying a variety of fruits instead of buying the same fruits many times.

Preparation

Set out the copies of page 84, scissors, trays and plastic coins on tables in preparation for group work.

Main teaching activity

Introduce the lesson to the class by explaining that they are going shopping at the fruit and vegetables stall. You are going to give them a set amount of money (for example, 20p), and they must fill their basket with fruit and vegetables to that value.

Ask the children to cut out or make the fruit and vegetables in preparation for the game. Start the game by saying: *You have 10p to spend, now fill your basket.* Groups of children

Linked to
L i t e r a c y
H i s t o r y

33 My timetable

Objectives

Numeracy
Understand and use the vocabulary related to time.
Order familiar events in time.
Read the time to the hour or half-hour on analogue clocks.
Solve simple problems set in 'real life' or measurement contexts.

Literacy
Read high-frequency words, including the days of the week.

History
Place events in chronological order.

Resources

A copy of photocopiable page 85 for each child, coloured felt-tip pens; a demonstration analogue clock.

Vocabulary

time
clock
hour
minute
big hand
little hand
morning
afternoon
evening
night
bedtime, playtime
today, yesterday, tomorrow
Monday, Tuesday...

Background

Year 1 children should know the names of the days of the week (see Lesson 15), know that there are seven days in a week and 24 hours in a day, and be able to read the time to the half hour and hour on an analogue clock. Discussing significant times in the children's day, including getting-up time, school start time, lunchtime, going home time, tea-time and bedtime, will help to develop their understanding of time measurement. The preparation of a simple personal timetable for the past week links to work in history and literacy on the order of events and the vocabulary of time.

Preparation

Set copies of page 85 and felt-tip pens on tables in preparation for the lesson. Set up the demonstration clock where it can be seen by the whole class.

Main teaching activity

Introduce the lesson by discussing the pattern of the children's day. *What time do you get up? What time do you leave for school? What time do you arrive home? What time do you go to bed? Are these times different at the weekend?* Use the demonstration clock to indicate the various times discussed.

Show the class the photocopiable sheet and explain that it is a personal timetable for them to complete. They should choose a colour code for each of the various activities listed, and colour in the appropriate hours. Ask the children to complete their own copies of the timetable sheet, guiding them to colour in the column for that particular day before considering how to complete the other days of the week.

Differentiation

Less able children should concentrate on colouring in the hours for the basic activities listed on the sheet: in bed, at school, playing and eating.

Encourage more able children to include additional activities on their timetable, such as playing with friends, helping at home or reading. Two spaces have been left on the key for the children's own activities.

Plenary

Make a display of some of the children's timetables and use this as a basis for discussion of the ways in which they use their time. *How many hours are you normally asleep each night? How many hours are you at school each day? Who gets up the earliest? Who goes to bed the latest?*

34 'I can play the...'

Background

Sorting and classifying activities arise in many areas of the curriculum, and particularly in science, ICT and mathematics. In Activity 16, the children sorted musical instruments as being string, wind or percussion, developing sorting and classifying skills in the contexts of music and science. This lesson develops the same theme: the children conduct a class survey of favourite instruments, presenting their results in the form of a simple block graph.

This lesson also links to work on sound and sound sources in music and science. Different instruments make different kinds of sound. Wind instruments produce sustained notes, varying from the pure tone of the recorder to the more 'reedy' sounds of the saxophone or oboe. Stringed instruments may be plucked (as in the guitar) or bowed (as in the violin). Percussion instruments produce a variety of sounds, from the boom of a bass drum to the crash of a cymbal.

Preparation

Make one copy per child of page 86 and cut out the pictures of instruments.

Main teaching activity

Introduce the lesson by reviewing the characteristics of the different classes of musical instrument, demonstrating the sounds that they make. Discuss with the children which instruments they think make the most exciting, sweetest, loudest, deepest, most interesting and clearest sounds. Ask the children about the musical instruments they play or would like to play. *Which is your favourite instrument?*

Explain that you are going to conduct a class survey of favourite musical instruments. Ask each child to choose his or her favourite

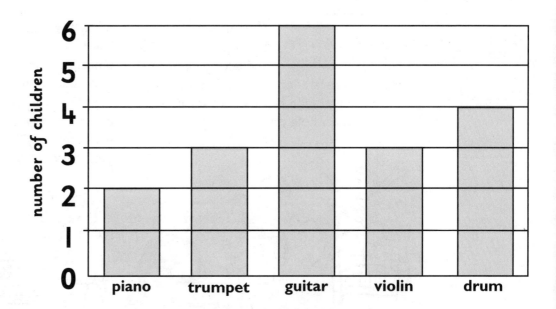

instrument and take the appropriate cut-out drawing from the photocopiable sheet. (If any children choose instruments not illustrated, they could draw them for themselves in blank rectangles. Have sheets of blank boxes ready for this purpose.) Now explain that you are going to make a kind of chart called a 'graph' to show the results of this survey. Collect the children's selected pictures and arrange the paper rectangles to make a simple block graph for classroom display. Label the graph as illustrated below.

Differentiation
Ask less able children to count the instruments represented by the blocks on the graph. *How many children chose the guitar as their favourite instrument?*

Ask more able children to sequence the choices. *Which was the most popular instrument? Which were the second and third most popular instruments?*

Plenary
Display the completed block graph on the wall. Discuss and plan similar surveys for other topics – the children's suggestions might include favourite foods, favourite pets, favourite colours and favourite school subjects.

35 Assessment 2

Preparation
Make copies of the assessment sheet before the lesson. If you feel that the sheet is too 'busy', the three activities could be separated and enlarged on individual sheets.

Lesson introduction
Begin the assessment lesson by reviewing the relevant cross-curricular topics covered during the term. Remind the children of some of the projects and investigations they have undertaken, and ask them to recall and recount their work. Emphasise the mathematical content – for example, *Do you remember how we wrote sums with both numbers and words?*

Main assessment activity
Distribute the sheets and ask the children to work on them individually. Guide the whole class through the questions one at a time, reading the text with them and prompting them to work out and fill in the answers. Try to make the whole activity enjoyable!

Practical activity
Set the hands on the clock face to show a time on the hour. Ask the child to tell the time. Repeat for several more 'on the hour' times, then extend to 'half past' times. Say a time on the hour or half-hour and ask the child to set the hands to the correct time.

Plenary
Review the answers to the questions as a class. Collect the completed assessment sheets to use as an aid to judging individual children's progress, and to include in your records. The answers are:

10p, 8p, 18p

Two add four equals six. (Or any equivalent statement.)
$3 + 4 = 7$

36 Secret codes

Objectives

Numeracy
Know the number names and recite them in order to at least 20, from and back to zero. Read and write numerals from 0 to at least 20.
Solve a given problem by sorting, classifying and organising information in simple ways.

Literacy
Practise and secure alphabetic letter knowledge and alphabetic order.

Resources
A whiteboard or flip chart, a marker pen. Paper, pencils.

Vocabulary
sequence
alphabet
code
order
first, second...
match

Background
The two most important sequences that children encounter in their early years education are the sequence of numbers and the sequence of letters of the alphabet. In this lesson, the children relate the two sequences through a simple 'secret code' activity. This numeracy lesson links to literacy work on the alphabet and alphabetical order.

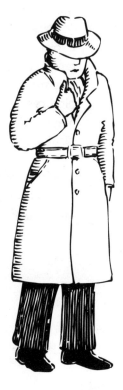

Preparation
Write the simple code below on the board or flip chart in preparation for the lesson.

Main teaching activity
Introduce the lesson with some counting and alphabet practice. Can the children say the number names to 26? Can they say the letters of the alphabet in sequence? Talk about sending secret messages. The children may be aware of methods used by spies and other characters in books, films and cartoons – for example, invisible ink and secret codes. Show the children the code you have written on the board and explain how it works. To write a secret message, numbers are substituted for the letters.

Write some simple words in code – for example, *3 1 20* or *4 15 7*, and ask the children to decipher them.

Write a selection of simple three-letter

and four-letter words on the board for the children to encode on paper. Then ask them to write their own names in code. Finally, suggest that they write a secret message to a friend in code. Pairs can then swap messages and decode them.

Differentiation
Children working at different levels will manage to encode and decode messages of different lengths.

Challenge the most able children to devise and use alternative codes – for example, numbering the letters in reverse order (a = 26, z = 1).

Plenary
As a class, look at and discuss some of the words, names and messages that the children have produced. *What are the numbers of the vowels? Which numbers appear most often in your messages? Which appear least often?*

a	b	c	d	e	f	g	h	i	j	k	l	m	n	o	p	q	r	s	t	u	v	w	x	y	z
1	2	3	4	5	6	7	8	9	10	11	12	13	14	15	16	17	18	19	20	21	22	23	24	25	26

Linked to History

37 My history book

Objectives

Numeracy
Know the number names and recite them in order to at least 20, from and back to zero.
History
Place events and objects in chronological order.
Find out about the past from a range of sources of information.
Ask and answer questions about the past.

Resources

A blank scrapbook (with 20 or more pages) for each child, pens, adhesive, scissors; magazines, photographs, old comics, posters and other printed materials from the past 20 years; a scrapbook for demonstration (see Preparation).

Vocabulary

year
one, two...
past
present

Background

Children in Year 1 are learning to count and compare numbers to 20, or at most 100. Timelines stretching over centuries have little meaning at this stage. Questions such as 'Were dinosaurs alive when you were a little girl, Miss?' reveal that the children are not yet ready to work with the large numbers needed to sequence distant historical events. However, they should begin to place recent events in chronological order (perhaps over a period of 20 years) and begin to appreciate that the past was different from the present.

Preparation

Prepare your own 20-year history scrapbook in advance of the lesson. This could be a history of the school using old photographs, a history of your family, a history of pop music, a history of a football team, or some similar theme of your choice. Label the first page '20 years ago', the next '19 years ago', and so on. Illustrate each page with relevant cuttings and pictures.

Main teaching activity

Introduce the main lesson with some practice in counting from zero to 20 and back again. Talk about the passing of the last 20 years. Encourage the children to compare this with their own ages and their memories of last year and the year before. Show the children your 20-year history scrapbook. Look through the pages and discuss the changes that have taken place during the period. Explain that the children are to make their own history scrapbooks, starting in this lesson. They should choose a theme for their history and collect pictures and cuttings to illustrate it.

Ask the children what themes they have chosen. Discuss each theme and make sure that it will be feasible to assemble a relevant scrapbook. Issue the blank scrapbooks and ask the children to label the pages in the same way that you have labelled your book. Together, make a start with sorting through the magazines and other resources that you have assembled to find illustrations for the children's histories.

Differentiation

More able children could assemble history scrapbooks covering a longer time period, such as 25 or 30 years.

Less able children could concentrate on the past 10 years only, perhaps making a scrapbook about their family or their favourite football team during that period.

Plenary

Review the children's progress with their scrapbooks, discussing where they might find additional material. Can their parents or grandparents help?

15 years ago   16 years ago

38 Playground robots

Objectives

Numeracy
Use everyday language to describe position, direction and movement.
Talk about things that turn.
Make whole turns and half turns.
PE
Remember and repeat simple skills and actions with increasing control and co-ordination.
ICT
Plan and give instructions to make things happen.
Links to QCA ICT Unit 1F.

Resources

A school hall or playground; plastic cones or other markers for simple tracks.

Vocabulary

turn
whole turn
half turn
quarter turn
forwards
backwards
left
right

Background

Programming floor robots such as PIP and Pixie requires children to distinguish the directions forwards, backwards, right and left. As they give movement instructions to the robot, they discover the link between the numbers input and the distances or amount of turn that result: bigger numbers produce proportionately bigger effects. As they program the robot to move, they will also discover how a list of commands or instructions can be issued to produce a desired result or to reach a pre-determined goal. The children should be introduced to, and work in small groups with, such robots throughout the year. A PE lesson in which the children role-play programmable robots is a good way to introduce the concepts involved.

Preparation

If possible, demonstrate the operation of a programmable robot to the whole class in advance of the lesson. Prepare for a PE lesson according to your normal practice.

Main teaching activity

Introduce the lesson with some simple moving and turning activities in which the whole class respond to your instructions. For example: *a whole turn right; a half turn left; a quarter turn right; one step forward; one step back; three steps forward; two steps back.*

Explain that the children are to work in pairs as 'robots and programmers'. They should take turns to act as the robot. The programmer issues instructions to make the robot move. Give the children several minutes to practise giving instructions and responding to them. Set out some simple tracks with cones or other markers, and challenge the pairs to take turns to guide their robot from the start to the finish.

Differentiation

Less able children could be given simple tracks involving no more than one or two turns and forward movements of two or three steps at a time.

More able children can be challenged with more demanding tracks to follow. Can they give the whole sequence of instructions before the robot sets off, rather than issuing one instruction at a time?

Plenary

Choose pairs to demonstrate their robot control skills to the whole class. Ask for a volunteer pair to guide the robot around a square, returning to the starting point.

Linked to
Literacy

39 Doubles & near doubles

Objectives

Numeracy
Know by heart addition doubles of all numbers to at least 5.
Identify near-doubles, using doubles already known.
Solve simple mathematical problems or puzzles; recognise and predict from simple patterns and relationships.
Explain methods and reasoning orally.
English (Speaking and listening)
Organise what they say.
Share ideas and experiences.
Take turns in speaking.

Resources

A whiteboard or flip chart and marker pen.

Vocabulary

double
near-double
add, more, make, sum, total, altogether
equals

Background

The ability to use doubles and near-doubles is very useful in making mental calculations. Children will soon come to know doubles of numbers to 5 by heart, and recognise near-doubles through frequent oral discussion of doubling in mental maths activities. Oral discussion of the strategies used to solve problems builds on the speaking and listening skills developed in English work.

Main teaching activity

Start the lesson by writing the numbers 1 to 10 on the board. Ask the children to double each number. *Double one is two, double two is four...* Write the sums $1 + 1 = 2$, $2 + 2 = 4$ and so on on the board as you discuss each double.

Ask the class a series of mental maths addition questions involving doubling, expressing them in a variety of ways. For example:

> **five plus five**
> **(answer: double five equals ten)**
>
> **double two**
> **(answer: double two equals four)**
>
> **I pick up three pencils, then three more. How many do I have?**
> **(answer: double three equals six)**

Develop the lesson by discussing near-doubles. Write these sums on the board:

Explain in each case that the sum is a double plus 1. For example, $4 + 5$ equals double 4 plus 1, which is 8 plus 1.

Ask the children a series of mental maths questions based on these near-doubles. For example:
- *Four plus five is how many?*
- *I have three coins in one hand and four in the other. How many coins do I have altogether?*

Ask the children to take turns to explain their answers, using the language of near-doubles that you have introduced. Prompt the children to ask questions if they do not understand an answer, and to share their ideas and methods with the whole class.

Differentiation

Less able children should concentrate on recalling doubles and near-doubles of numbers to 5.

More able children can work with doubles and near-doubles of numbers to 10 and beyond.

Plenary

Conclude the lesson with some quick-fire doubling and near doubling mental maths questions: *double three; 5 plus 5; 3 add 4*; and so on.

40 Treasure Island

Objectives

Numeracy
Use everyday language to describe position, direction and movement.

Geography
Identify and describe where places are. Make maps and plans (for example, a pictorial map of a place in a story).

Resources

A large sand tray; various models and toys (such as houses, trees and boats) to create an island scene; some 'treasure' (such as a miniature toy treasure chest); a lolly stick and pen for each child.

Vocabulary

next to
underneath
between
in front, behind
beside
opposite

Background

The vocabulary of position is developed in practical contexts when children hear and talk about objects that are *in the middle* of the floor, *on top of* the cupboard, *next to* the chair, *underneath* the table, *opposite* the door, *inside* the box and so on. In this activity, the children use the sand tray to play a treasure hunt game that develops their understanding and use of this vocabulary. The activity links to sentence-level work in literacy, and to work on locations and their description in geography.

Preparation

Smooth the surface of the sand in the tray and bury the 'treasure' when the children are not looking. Distribute the lolly sticks and ask each child to write his or her name on a stick.

Main teaching activity

Gather the class around the sand tray and explain that you are going to create an island scene. With the children's help, use the models and toys to create a desert island. Now explain that you have reason to believe there is treasure buried on the island. The children's task is to guess where this treasure might be. Let them take turns to choose a location and describe it to you – for example: 'I think the treasure might be behind the house, next to the tree.' Plant the child's stick in the location described, continuing the discussion and use of position words as you place the stick: *Here, or more to the right?* Continue until all the children have planted their name sticks.

Differentiation

The children's abilities will be differentiated by their use of position vocabulary as they describe their chosen location. You could develop the activity by challenging more able children to draw a treasure map and write an imaginative description, perhaps in the form of a story, of where the treasure is buried.

Plenary

Let the children take turns to dig beneath their sticks to see whether they can find the treasure. Review the description of each location as the children are digging.

Linked to
S c i e n c e

41 How much does it hold?

Objectives

Numeracy
Compare two capacities by direct comparison; extend to more than two. Measure using uniform non-standard units. Record estimates and measurements as 'about 3 beakers full'.

Science
Make and record observations and measurements.

Resources

A water tray; a selection of plastic bottles, yoghurt pots, beakers and other containers; sticky labels, pens; plastic funnels.

Vocabulary

full
half-full
empty
holds
container
measure

Background

In Year 1, many children will only just be starting to understand that the volume of a liquid is conserved (stays the same) as the liquid is poured from one container to another. Some children may still think that there is 'more' in a tall thin container than in a short broad one, because the shape of the liquid is taller. Comparing the capacities of different-sized and different-shaped containers by pouring from one to another, and measurement using cups or yoghurt pots as measures, will help the children to develop conservation concepts. This mathematics lesson links closely to work on materials and measurement in science.

Preparation

Set out the water tray and plastic items in preparation for the lesson.

Main teaching activity

Select two different-shaped plastic bottles of similar capacity. Ask the children which bottle they think holds more. Can they suggest a way to check their prediction? Show the children how to compare the capacities of the bottles directly: fill one bottle to the brim and empty it into the second bottle, using the funnel if necessary. Discuss whether or not the first bottle has a greater capacity than the second bottle. Set the children to work in groups to compare similar-sized containers in the same way.

When the children have understood how to make direct comparisons, explain how they can use a small yoghurt pot as a measure to compare the capacities of a whole range of containers. Select a bottle and ask the children to predict how many cups or pots of water it will hold. Check their estimates practically by pouring in potfuls of water and counting until the bottle is full. Set the groups to estimate and then measure the capacities of a variety of containers, using a yoghurt pot measure. They could label each container with its measured capacity.

Differentiation

Less able children should concentrate on making direct comparisons between pairs of containers.

Challenge more able children to estimate the capacities (in yoghurt pot units) of a variety of containers, place them in order of how much they hold and then check their predictions by measuring with a yoghurt pot.

Plenary

Ask representatives of the different groups to hold up some of the containers they have measured and describe their findings. Encourage the use of the vocabulary of comparison: *more than, less than, bigger, smaller* and so on.

42 Circle dance

Background

Many children's games and dances involve joining hands in a circle. 'Ring-a-Ring-a-Roses', 'The Farmer's In His Den' and 'The Hokey-Cokey' are familiar examples. As they play these games, children turn together and individually; they go in and out, sit down, stand up and turn about. Taking part in such games and dances provides an excellent link between the mathematics and vocabulary of shape and movement and the physical activity of PE and dance.

Preparation

Prepare the class for a PE lesson in the hall or playground according to your normal practice.

Main teaching activity

Introduce the lesson by using PE hoops to talk about the properties of circles. Ask the children what shape a hoop is. Let them trace the circumference (there's no need to introduce the word at this stage) of a hoop with their hands. Compare the actions of rolling the hoop and turning it in another direction. Ask the children to roll their hoops across the floor. Can any of the children step through a hoop as it is rolling? Lay the hoops on the ground and ask the children to: walk around the hoop; step into the hoop; make a whole turn inside the hoop; make a half turn inside the hoop; step out of the hoop; and so on.

Once you have completed the hoop activities, develop the vocabulary of circles and turning with some circle games and dances such as those listed in Background.

Differentiation

All of the children can take part in the dances and games. You could challenge more able children to measure how far a hoop travels in a single turn. They will need to mark a point on the circumference of the hoop with sticky tape, then observe the point moving round as the hoop is rolled. *Do big hoops travel further than small hoops?*

Plenary

Conclude the lesson with a short discussion of other things that are circular or turn round. The children might suggest coins, biscuits, wheels, fairground rides and so on. Emphasise that all these things can be described using the words 'circle', 'circular' or 'turning in a circle', illustrating a circle with your hand as you do so.

43 Shape spotting

Objectives

Numeracy
Use everyday language to describe features of familiar 3-D and 2-D shapes, including the cube, cuboid, sphere, cylinder, cone, circle, triangle, square and rectangle, referring to properties such as the shapes of flat faces, the number of faces or corners, or the number and types of sides.
Begin to relate solid shapes to pictures of them.

Geography
Make observations about where things are located.
Links to QCA Geography Unit 1.

Resources

A copy of photocopiable page 88 for each child; large sheets of display paper; magazines and newspapers with pictures of buildings and scenes of the environment; scissors, adhesive, felt-tip pens.

Vocabulary

triangle
circle
square
rectangle
star
cube
cuboid
pyramid
sphere
hemisphere
cone
cylinder

Background

The children's environment is full of shapes with mathematical names. Road signs and windows are circles, triangles, rectangles and squares. Bricks and many buildings are cuboids; chimneys are cylinders; domes are hemispheres. Identifying and describing shapes in the environment links mathematics to geography work in which the children investigate their immediate surroundings.

Preparation

Copy the worksheets and distribute them on desks with the other materials in preparation for the lesson.

Main teaching activity

Start the lesson by looking at the photocopiable sheet. Can the children identify and colour the shapes shown in the scene? Explain that the word list at the bottom of the sheet contains the names of the shapes. Suggest that they choose a different colour for each type of shape – for example, colouring squares red, circles blue, triangles yellow and so on. Review the shapes the children have identified.

Continue the lesson by discussing shapes in the school environment and the immediate surroundings. Can the children recall and describe examples of rectangles, triangles, circles, cylinders and other shapes?

Explain that you are going to create a shape display on the classroom wall. Label display sheets with shape headings: *squares, circles, triangles* and so on. Ask the children to find pictures of objects in magazines and newspapers that have the various shapes, then cut them out and stick them to the display sheets. They could work in groups, each group searching for examples of a particular shape or shapes.

Differentiation

Less able children can concentrate on basic 2-D shapes such as circles and rectangles.

Challenge more able children to identify 3-D shapes such as cones, cylinders and pyramids.

Plenary

Review the shape display with the class, asking children to identify the different objects and describe their shapes.

44 How many animals?

Background

A model farmyard with groups of plastic animals is a valuable resource for imaginative play in the classroom. Sets of plastic animals can be used to develop children's estimation and counting skills for numbers to 30. Groups of different animals are described by different collective nouns: a **herd** of cows or horses, a **flock** of sheep or pigeons, a **gaggle** of geese, a **school** of whales, a **shoal** of fish, a **swarm** of bees, a **pack** of wolves, an **army** of ants, a **plague** of locusts, a **pride** of lions. A numeracy lesson based on estimation of animal numbers can be linked to work in literacy on building up vocabulary to describe animal and other groupings.

Preparation

Set out the plastic animals on tables in preparation for the lesson.

Main teaching activity

The children will have started to develop their estimation skills in previous lessons (for example, see lessons 11 and 21). In this lesson, they can work in threes to challenge each other in an estimation game.

Introduce the lesson by talking about animal groupings, introducing some of the collective nouns listed above (see Background). Discuss how a good farmer or shepherd can estimate accurately the number of animals in a herd or flock. A good way to do this is by trying to 'see' the animals in groups of five (most children can see that a group contains five things without counting them one by one), then counting the number of fives.

Show the children how to play the following game. One child sets out a group of plastic animals behind a card so that they are hidden from the other two children. The first child then lifts the card. The two observers must call out their estimate of the number of animals, and name the animal grouping, together. The animals are then counted, and the child with the closest estimate wins the chance to set out the next animal group.

Let the groups start by playing the game with up to 10 animals at a time, then increase the maximum number to 20 and finally 30.

Differentiation

Less able groups should work with animal numbers up to 20.

More able children could progress to estimating up to 30, then 50 animals.

Plenary

Play the game with the whole class, discussing the estimation strategies the children have developed. Did they find it easy to estimate by counting in fives, or did they prefer grouping in some other number?

Objectives

Numeracy
Understand and use the vocabulary of estimation.
Give a sensible estimate of a number of objects that can be checked by counting (eg up to about 30 objects).
Literacy
Learn new words from reading and shared experiences, and make collections of words linked to particular topics.

Resources

Sets of plastic farm (or other) animals; sheets of card.

Vocabulary

estimate
about
guess how many
too many, too few
just over, just under

100 CROSS-CURRICULAR MATHS LESSONS Years 1 & 2/Scottish Primary 1–3

45 Time of day

Background

At this stage, children should be reading times to the nearest hour and half-hour from an analogue clock. They should be using the 12-hour clock and the terms 'am' and 'pm' to express times of day. Ordering familiar events through the day along a timeline marked in hours practises both sequencing and time-measurement skills. This work links to work in history in which children start to order events in chronological sequence. Developing a timeline for a single day introduces historical thinking in a context that young children readily understand.

Preparation

Distribute copies of page 89 on tables in advance of the lesson.

Main teaching activity

Introduce the lesson by discussing the passing of time during the day and the events that take place at different times. As you rotate the hands on the clock face, ask the children to raise their hands when you reach getting-up time and other significant points. Ask them at what times they leave for school, enter the classroom, start each lesson, break for playtime and so on.

Show the children the photocopiable sheet. Explain that the children should link the events named in the boxes to the appropriate points on the timeline for their own typical day. Encourage them to check their answers by thinking through the order of events in their day.

Differentiation

All children should locate the regular school events quoted (assembly, playtimes, lunchtime and home time) accurately on the timeline. Less able children should locate their personal events to the nearest hour.

Encourage more able children to locate events to the nearest half-hour, or still more precisely.

Plenary

As a class, compare and contrast some of the completed timelines. Discuss the variation in times such as getting-up time and bedtime. Develop the topic by considering how a timeline might be extended over several days, months or years. *What kind of events could we show on a timeline for a year?* (Birthdays, holidays, seasonal changes and so on.)

46 Robot run

Objectives

Numeracy
Understand and use the vocabulary of comparing and ordering numbers.
Understand the operations of addition and subtraction, and use the related vocabulary.

ICT
Explore a variety of ICT tools.
Plan and give instructions to make things happen.
Links to QCA ICT Unit 1F.

Resources

A programmable floor robot such as PIP or Pixie; a suitable number track, grid or maze for the robot to move in.

Vocabulary

number line
forwards, backwards
along
count on
count back
add
subtract
take away

Background

Programming a floor robot or turtle provides numerous opportunities for developing number and spatial skills, knowledge of angles and problem-solving strategies. In this lesson, the children develop their knowledge of the 0–30 number line by programming a floor robot to reach different positions on the line. The activity could be performed equally well through role-play of the robot movements (see Lesson 39), or by moving a turtle on a computer screen. Work with programmable robots and screen turtles also develops the children's ICT skills: they learn to produce a desired result by issuing a sequence of instructions.

Preparation

Prepare a suitable number track (with the numbers spaced by, for example, 20cm) in advance of the lesson. Set up the robot so that its unit of linear movement (forward 1 or back 1) corresponds to the spacing between the numbers on your track. You will find the necessary instructions for setting up the robot in the robot's user manual.

Main teaching activity

Start the lesson with whole-class counting, addition and subtraction practice based on the number track you have set out. Introduce the robot to the class, explaining how it can be 'told' (programmed) to move forwards or backwards a set number of steps with

instructions such as 'Forward 3' or 'Back 2'.

Place the robot at the start of the track. Ask the children what instruction you need to give in order to make the robot travel to a specific number. Let them take turns to press the keys, instructing the robot to move to a selection of different locations. Use the vocabulary of movement, addition and subtraction as you describe where the robot should go next – for example, with the robot on 6, say *Now he wants to go to 10, 10 is 4 more than 6, 6 plus 4 equals 10, so we must enter 'Forward 4'*. As the lesson develops, encourage the children to explain their reasoning in a similar way.

Differentiation

Ask less able children to give a single instruction to move the robot forwards or backwards, relating the movement to the addition or subtraction of two numbers.

More able children can be challenged to issue a sequence of two or more instructions corresponding to the addition or subtraction of three or more numbers. You could position a series of markers on the number track (coloured flags, for example) for the robot to visit in a sequence.

Plenary

Conclude the lesson with some quick-fire questions. Ask individual children to role-play the robot by pointing to various numbers on the track as you issue a sequence of instructions: *Forward 10, back 3, forward 7...*

47 Slot machine

Objectives

Numeracy
Recognise coins of different values.
Find totals and change from up to 20p.
Work out how to pay an exact sum using smaller coins.

Design and technology
Investigate and evaluate a range of familiar products.
Carry out design and make assignments using a range of materials.

Resources

Card boxes, coloured paper, scissors, adhesive, felt-tip pens; plastic coins; items for the 'machines' to dispense (for example disposable plastic cups).

Vocabulary

money
coin
penny, pence
price
cost
buy
pay
change

Background

Children find slot machines selling drinks, confectionery or tickets fascinating. They love to select an item, insert the coins and watch the mechanism operate. Some machines give change, while others require the exact money. To operate such a machine, children need to read the price and work out how to pay it using a combination of coins. In this activity, the children make and 'operate' their own model slot machines to practise these numeracy and money skills. Constructing and decorating the machines uses design and technology skills.

Preparation

Set out the materials on tables and prepare the children according to your normal practice for a design and technology lesson.

Main teaching activity

Introduce the lesson by talking about slot machines that the children have used. *Where have you used a ticket machine? Have you used a drinks machine or a chocolate machine – for example, at the local swimming pool? Do the machines give change, or do you need to insert the exact money?*

Explain that the children are going to make their own slot machines. They could choose, for example, to make a drinks machine or a ticket machine. Before they start, they should think about how the machine will work. *Will it give change? How many different items will it give out? How*

the customer choose which item to buy? Suggest that the children could make a simple machine like the one shown below, with a separate slot for each purchase. Encourage them to develop their own ideas. Explain that each 'machine' will be operated by a child sitting behind the box.

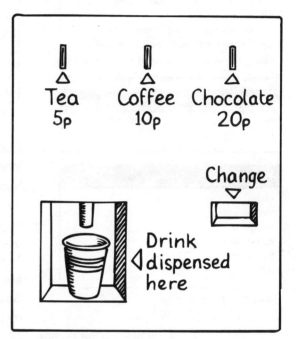

Ask the children to work in groups, building slot machines. When they have finished their machine, they should operate it: some children will role-play customers by selecting purchases and inserting coins through the slots, while other children operate the machine from behind by counting the coins fed in and dispensing purchased items and change.

Differentiation

Less able children should construct a simple machine to dispense one of two or three items when the exact money is inserted.

More able children could develop their own ideas to produce more complex machines.

Plenary

Ask the groups to explain and demonstrate the various machines they have designed and built.

48 Library books

Objectives

Numeracy
Use mental strategies to solve simple problems set in 'real life' contexts.
Compare two lengths by direct comparison.
Solve a given problem by sorting, classifying and organising information in simple ways.
Literacy
Practise and secure alphabetic order.
Use the terms 'fiction' and 'non-fiction', noting some of their differing features.

Resources

A selection of books, magazines and comics for sorting.

Vocabulary

order
size
compare
between
bigger, smaller
next

Background

Within a library or a bookshop, various strategies are used to sort and arrange books on the shelves. Fiction and non-fiction are usually separated. Books and journals may be arranged by subject, issue number, publication date, author, title or size. The sorting and sequencing skills needed to find or place books on the shelves build on mathematical and linguistic knowledge. In this lesson, the children use numeracy skills to sort books, magazines and comics by date, size or number of pages. They also use literacy skills to sort these publications by subject, author or title.

Preparation

Distribute the items to be sorted on tables in advance of the lesson.

Main teaching activity

Introduce the lesson by discussing how books and magazines are organised in the school library. *Where are the fiction books kept? Where are the non-fiction books kept? Are big books and small books kept in separate places? Are books about different subjects arranged separately from each other? What order are the books on one subject arranged in?*

Talk about different ways of sorting, both **numerical** (for example, comics and magazines) and **alphabetic** (for example, author names). Extend the discussion to local bookshops and libraries that the children have visited.

Show the children the books, magazines and comics you have selected for them to sort. Discuss various strategies for sorting, and ask the children to work in groups of three or four to complete some sorting activities. For example, ask one group to sort a pile of magazines by month of issue, a second group to sort a pile of books into fiction and non-fiction, a third group to sort a pile of fiction books into alphabetical order by author's name, a fourth group to sort a pile of non-fiction books by subject, and so on.

Differentiation

Less able children could sort a selection of books by size (either height or width, as they prefer).

Challenge more able children to sort a pile of books, magazines or comics by publication date or number of pages.

Plenary

Ask a representative of each group to show the results of the group's sorting and explain the strategy they have used. In a follow-up activity, the class could visit the school library or local public library to investigate how the books are arranged on the shelves.

Linked to
S c i e n c e

49 My measuring scale

Objectives

Numeracy
Measure using uniform non-standard units.
Science
Recognise and compare the main external parts of the bodies of humans.
Links to QCA Science Unit 1A.

Resources

One copy per child of photocopiable page 90, scissors, adhesive, pencils; two rulers of different lengths, marked in centimetres.

Vocabulary

ruler
measure
length
size
compare
unit
standard
centimetre
inch

Background

Many traditional measuring units were originally based on parts of the human body. An inch was the length of the top joint of an adult thumb; the hand (still used to measure the height of horses) was the width of a hand; the foot was the length of a foot; the yard was the length of an adult pace; the cubit (the unit in which the dimensions of Noah's Ark are given in the Bible) was the distance from the elbow to the tip of the outstretched index finger. Of course, these dimensions vary from person to person, and these units were eventually standardised before being superseded by the metric system. In Year 1, children can use their own body parts as non-standard measuring units to make and compare measurements. This links to their awareness of their own bodies in science work.

Preparation

Make copies of page 90 on card, or make the card strips from the sheet, and place them on tables in advance of the lesson.

Main teaching activity

Introduce the lesson by discussing body-based measuring units, in particular the inch. Explain that the inch is an old-fashioned measure of length that was originally based on the length of the top part of the thumb. Show the children how to measure the length of their lower arm, from elbow to fingertip, with the top joint of the thumb. Ask all the children to make this measurement. Compare their answers.

Explain that the children are going to make their own ruler for measuring, based on 'thumb' units. Demonstrate how to set out and number a scale of thumb lengths on a card strip.

Ask the children to make their 'thumb rulers' individually from the sheet (or from card strips). When these are completed, the children can use them to measure the dimensions of their own body – for example, the length of their hands, feet and arms.

Differentiation

Less able children should concentrate on making and using their own ruler.

Challenge more able children to compare their measurements and rulers and discuss the extent of the differences.

Plenary

Compare the rulers produced by different children. Talk about the differences: different children have different-sized thumbs. Discuss the problems this might cause if the 'thumb' was used as a measure for making a house or a car. Explain that the rulers we use are not made like that: they use **standard** units called **centimetres**. Compare two different-length centimetre rulers and show that 1cm is the same on both.

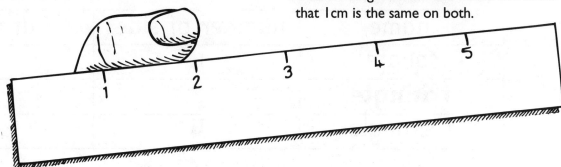

50 Assessment 3

Preparation

Make copies of the assessment sheet in advance of the lesson. If you feel that the sheet is too 'busy', the three activities could be separated and enlarged on individual sheets.

Lesson introduction

Begin the assessment lesson by reviewing the relevant cross-curricular topics covered during the term. Remind the children of some of the projects and investigations they have undertaken, and ask them to recall and recount their work. Emphasise the mathematical content – for example, *Do you remember how we programmed the robot to move forward, move backwards and turn round?*

Main assessment activity

Distribute the sheets and ask the children to work on them individually. Guide the whole class through the questions one at a time, reading the text with them and prompting them to work out and fill in the answers. Try to make the whole activity enjoyable!

Practical activity

Pull different 2-D shapes from the box and ask the child to name them. Name a shape and ask the child to find it in the box. Ask

the child to describe the shape that he or she has picked out. Ask the child to create a repeating line of shapes – for example: triangle, square, triangle, square...

Plenary

Review the answers to the questions as a class. Collect the completed question sheets to use as an aid to judging individual children's progress, and to include in your records. The answers are:

four, red

Objectives

The assessment activities in this book are designed to introduce Key Stage 1 children to SAT-style questions. They are set in cross-curricular contexts based on the preceding term's lessons. The questions in Assessment 3 test children's progress in: interpreting simple block graphs; following movement instructions; and classifying shapes.

Resources

One copy per child of photocopiable page 91, pencils; a box of basic 2-D shapes.

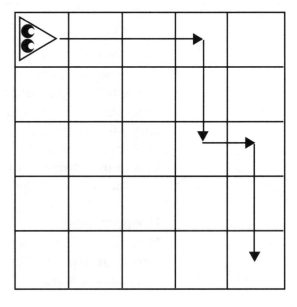

name	number of sides	drawing
square	4	▢
triangle	3	△
rectangle	4	▭

Football shirts

- Can you design 6 different shirts using just 3 colours?
- Use no more than 2 colours per shirt.

SCHOLASTIC

Record breakers

● Match each animal to the record it holds.
  One has been done for you.

tallest land animal

heaviest land animal

biggest animal ever

fastest land animal

biggest land animal ever

Tangram puzzle

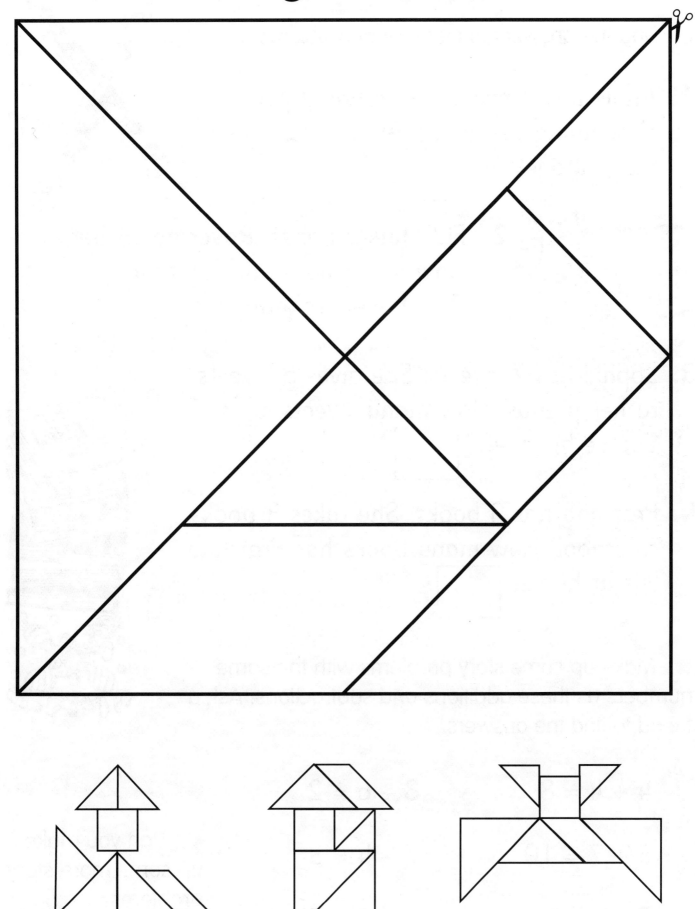

Story problems

● Find the answers to these story problems.

1. Annie has 4 pencils. Tom has 2 pencils.
   How many pencils do Annie and Tom
   have altogether? ☐

2. Fido has 3 bones. Rover has 5 bones.
   How many bones do Rover and
   Fido have altogether? ☐

3. Sophie has 7 sweets. She gives 5 sweets
   to her friends. How many sweets does
   Sophie have left? ☐

4. Prarthna has 9 books. She takes 3 books
   to school. How many books has Prarthna
   left at home? ☐

● Make up some story problems with the same
numbers as these additions and subtractions. Ask a
friend to find the answers.

$$4 + 4 = 8 \qquad 8 - 6 = 2$$

$$3 + 7 = 10 \qquad 7 - 4 = 3$$

● Can you make
up some more story
problems?

$$5 + 4 = 9 \qquad 6 - 1 = 5$$

Number necklaces

● Fill in the gaps.

T	U	
	I	one
I	0	ten
I	I	

Number ladder

Instructions

1. Cut out the ladder and the spinners.
2. Stick the spinners onto card. Push a stick through the middle.
3. Put your counters on the 0 rung of the ladder.
4. Take turns to spin both spinners.
5. Move your counter by plus (+) or minus (–) the number you score. If that would take you below 0, wait for another turn.
6. The first player to reach 20 wins.

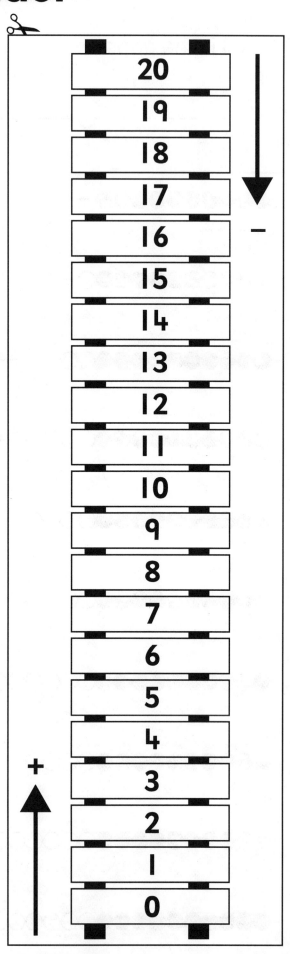

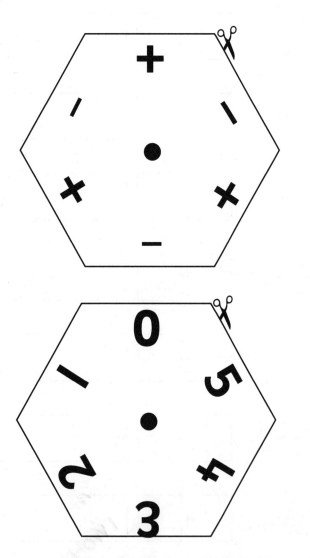

Shopping

pencil sharpener 10p

crayon 3p

note book 8p

NOTES

ruler 4p

- How much are:

1. A paper clip and a ruler? ☐

2. A pencil and a notebook? ☐

3. A ruler and a rubber? ☐

4. A pencil sharpener and a ruler? ☐

5. A crayon, a ruler and a rubber? ☐

6. A pencil sharpener, a notebook and a paper clip?

- How much change do you get from 20p for:

pencil 2p

paper clip 1p

rubber 5p

7. A crayon? ☐

8. A notebook? ☐

9. A notebook and a pencil? ☐

10. A ruler and a pencil sharpener? ☐

11. A pencil sharpener, a notebook and a paper clip? ☐

■SCHOLASTIC

Name

● Fill in the missing house numbers.

1	3		7		11		

2		6			12		

● How much money does Sophie have?

1p

5p

2p

_____ p

● How much money does Sunita have?

2p

1p

2p

10p

5p

_____ p

● Draw an arrow to show which set each instrument belongs to.

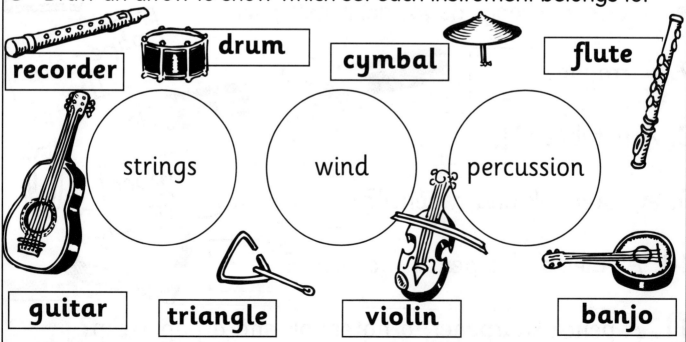

recorder

drum

cymbal

flute

strings

wind

percussion

guitar

triangle

violin

banjo

Dot-to-dot puzzle

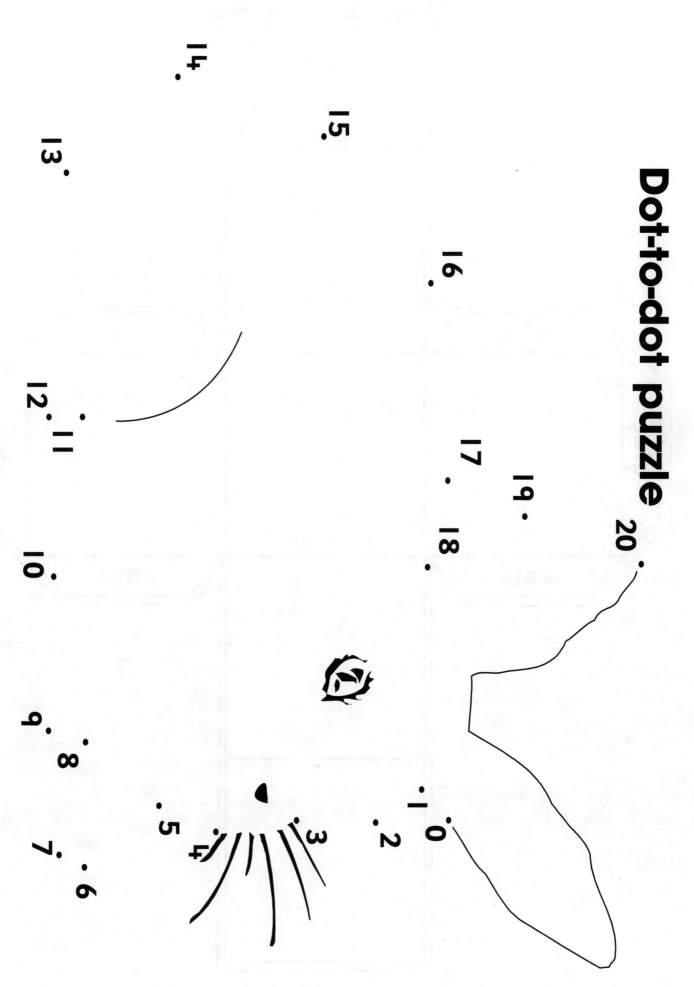

Make a dice

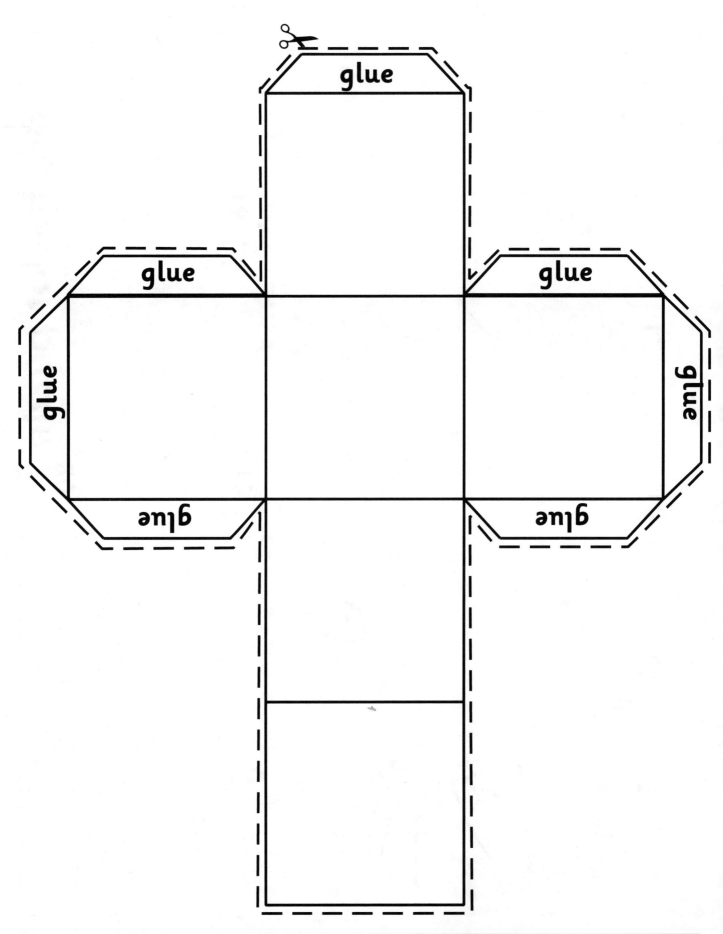

Addition words and symbols

add	plus	sum
total	totals	make
makes	equal	equals
is	the	of
and	are	together
altogether	more	gives
+	**=**	**+**

■▲SCHOLASTIC

Addition sentences

● Match the words and numerals.

three plus four equals seven

two plus eight gives ten

$2 + 4 = 6$

$5 + 3 = 8$

$3 + 6 = 9$

two and four more total six

five add three makes eight

$2 + 8 = 10$

$3 + 4 = 7$

three and six make nine altogether

Shape patterns

● Name the pattern.

circle, square

Symmetry test

● Which shapes are symmetrical?
● Cut out each shape and fold it in half to see.

Dominoes

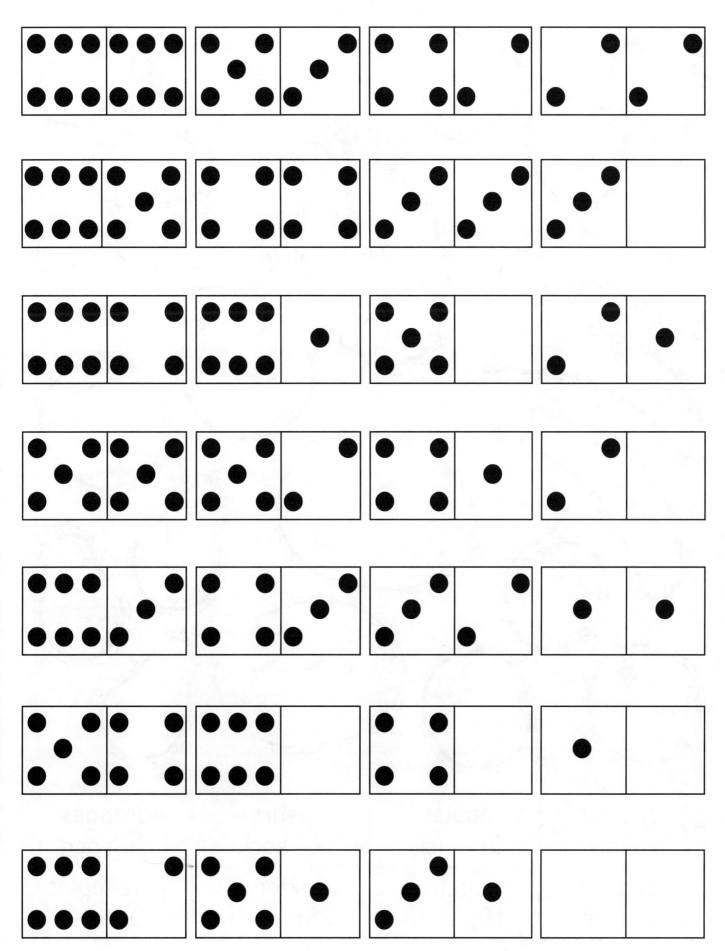

Fill your basket

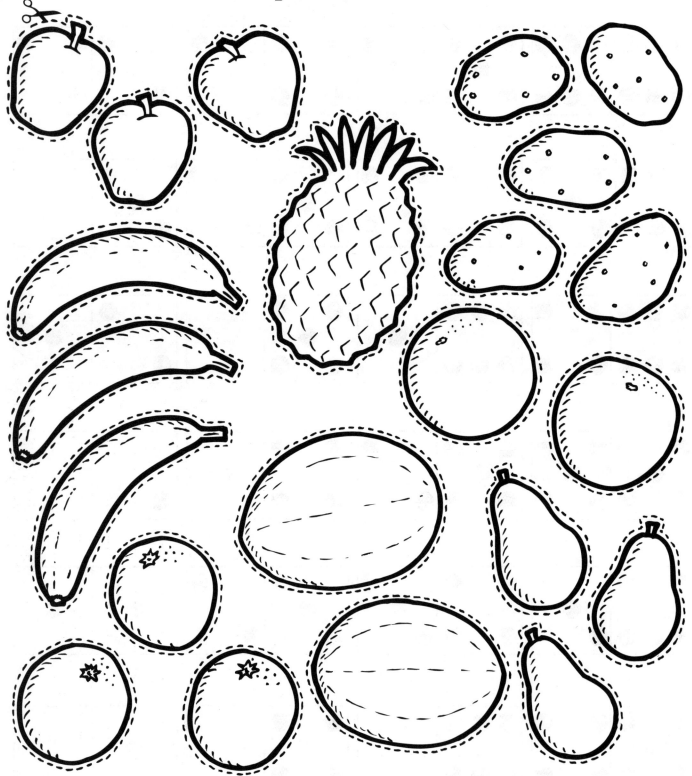

potatoes 1p each	apples 2p each	pears 2p each	oranges 3p each
bananas 5p each	grapefruit 10p each	melons 15p each	pineapples 20p each

My timetable

	Monday	Tuesday	Wednesday	Thursday	Friday	Saturday	Sunday
5 o'clock							
6 o'clock							
7 o'clock							
8 o'clock							
9 o'clock							
10 o'clock							
11 o'clock							
12 noon							
1 o'clock							
2 o'clock							
3 o'clock							
4 o'clock							
5 o'clock							
6 o'clock							
7 o'clock							
8 o'clock							
9 o'clock							
10 o'clock							

in bed

in school

playing

eating

I can play the...

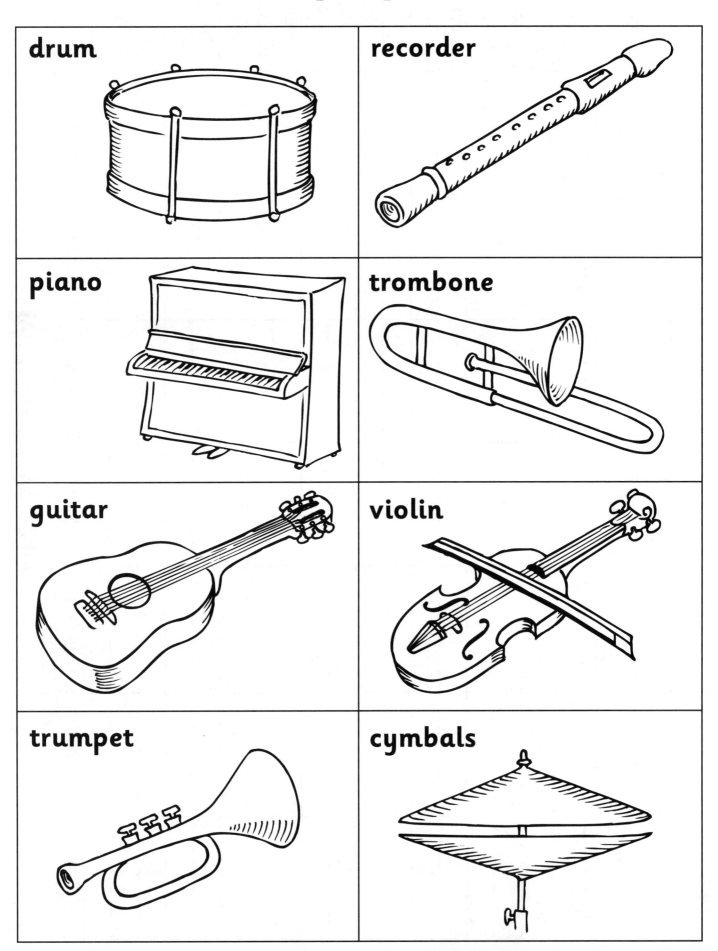

drum

recorder

piano

trombone

guitar

violin

trumpet

cymbals

Name

● How much do these stamps cost?

| _____ p | | _____ p |

● all of them together | _____ p |

● Write this sum in words.

2 + 4 = 6 | Two |

● Write this sentence using numbers and symbols.

Three add four equals seven. | |

● Draw hands on these clocks to show the times written below them.

six o'clock   three o'clock   half past nine

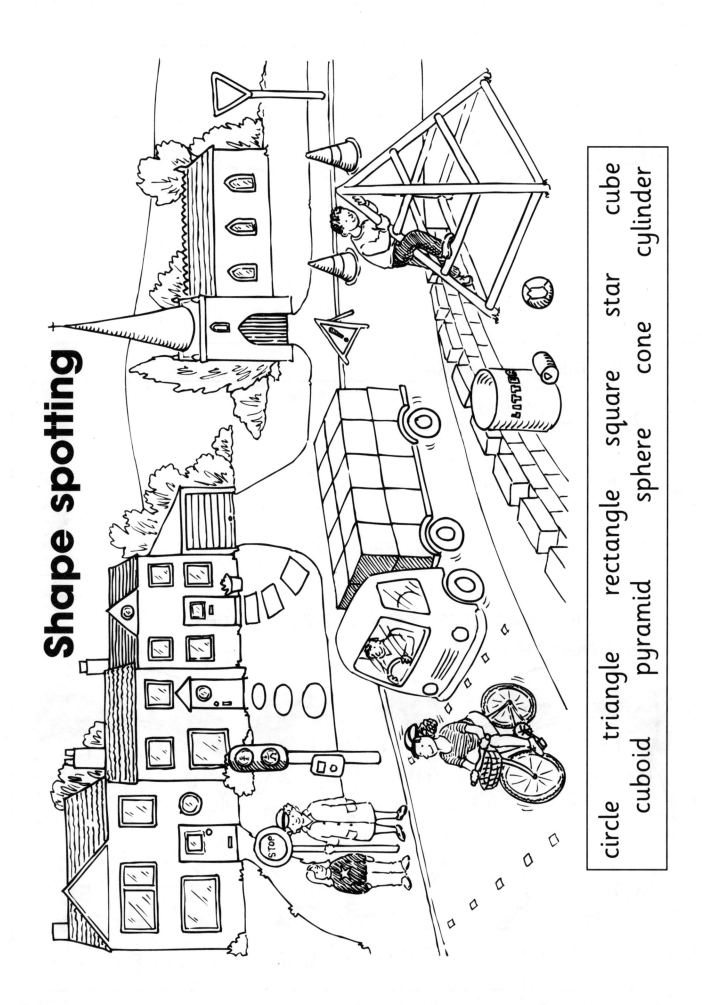

Shape spotting

circle   triangle   rectangle   square   star   cube
cuboid   pyramid   sphere   cone   cylinder

My timeline

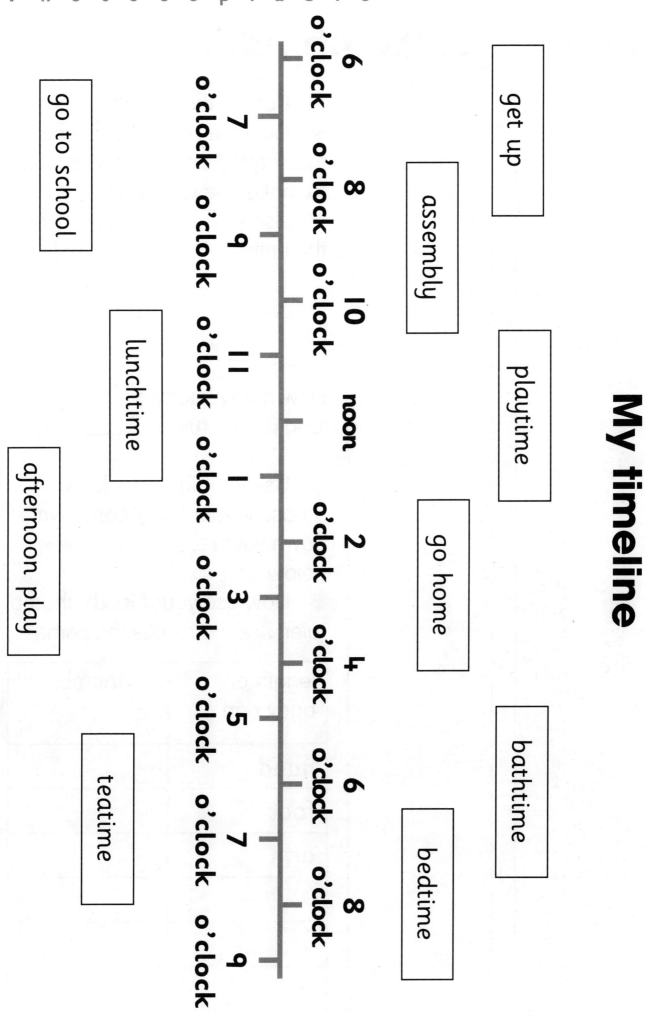

get up

assembly

playtime

go home

bathtime

bedtime

go to school

lunchtime

afternoon play

teatime

6 o'clock
7 o'clock
8 o'clock
9 o'clock
10 o'clock
11 o'clock
noon
1 o'clock
2 o'clock
3 o'clock
4 o'clock
5 o'clock
6 o'clock
7 o'clock
8 o'clock
9 o'clock

■SCHOLASTIC

Glue here

A thumb ruler

● Cut out the two strips.
● Glue the second strip onto the shaded part of the first strip to make one long strip.
● Use your thumb to mark out the units.

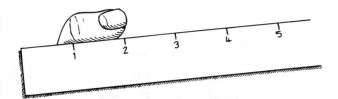

How many 'thumbs' long is your ruler? _____

● Use your thumb ruler to measure your body parts. Write down your results in the table below.
● Now use your friend's thumb ruler. Are the results the same?

length of body part	'thumbs'
hand	
foot	
arm	

Name

● Some children made a survey of their favourite colours.

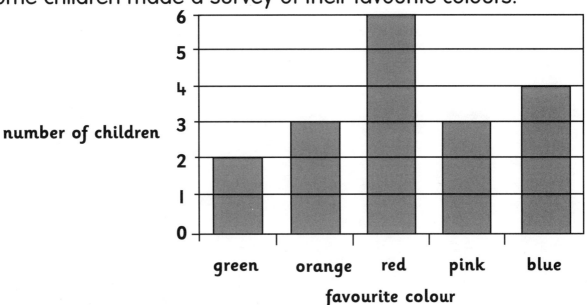

number of children

favourite colour

● How many children chose blue?

● Which was the most popular colour?

The robot follows these instructions:

> forward 3
> right
> forward 2
> left
> forward 1
> right
> forward 2

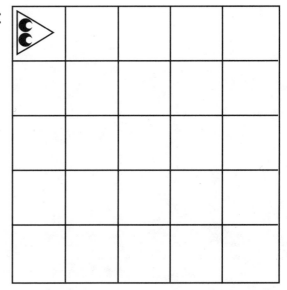

● Draw its track on the grid.

● Fill in the gaps in this table.

name	number of sides	drawing
square		☐
	3	△
rectangle		▭

100
Cross-curricular
Maths
Lessons

Lesson plans and photocopiable activity pages

Year 2

Planning Grid

Term 1	Topics	Maths objectives	Cross-curricular objectives	Activities
Unit 1	Counting and properties of numbers	Say the number names in order to at least 100, from and back to zero. Count in hundreds from and back to zero; count on in twos from and back to zero or any small number, and recognise odd and even numbers to at least 30; count on in steps of 3, 4 or 5 to least 30, from and back to zero, then from and back to any given small number.	**Physical education** Explore basic skills, actions and ideas with increasing understanding. Remember and repeat simple skills and actions with increasing control and co-ordination. Links with QCA PE Games activities Unit 2.	**p.97: Count the skips** In a PE lesson, count skips in ones, twos, fives, tens...
2–4	Place value and ordering Understanding + and – Mental calculation strategies (+ and –) Money and 'real-life' problems Making decisions and checking results	Describe and extend simple number sequences: count on or back in ones or tens, starting from any two-digit number; count in twos from and back to zero or any small number, and recognise odd and even numbers to at least 30; count on in steps of 3,4 or 5 to at least 30, from and back to zero. Begin to recognise two-digit multiples of 2, 5 or 10.	**Information technology** To plan and give instructions to make things happen. Links to QCA IT Units 2B and 2D.	**p.98: Make a pattern** Use a 100 grid or the computer to create repeating patterns by colouring every second, third, fifth, tenth square...
		Extend understanding of the operations of addition and subtraction. Use and begin to read the related vocabulary. Use the +, – and = signs to record mental additions and subtractions in a number sentence, and recognise the use of a symbol such as ? or ? to stand for an unknown number.	**ICT** Explore a variety of ICT tools. To use text and images to develop their ideas. To try things out and explore what happens. Links to QCA IT Unit 2A.	**p.99: Calculate that! 1** Use a computer to practise addition and subtraction to 20.
5–6	Measures – including problems Shape and space Reasoning about shapes	Use and begin to read the vocabulary of comparing and ordering numbers, including ordinal. Use and begin to read the vocabulary related to time. Know the days of the week.	**Literacy** To read on sight high-frequency words including days of the week.	**p.100: Days of the week** Use ordinal numbers to label the days of the week. Which is the first day of the school week?
		Use and begin to read the vocabulary of estimation and approximation; give a sensible estimate of at least 50 objects.	**Geography** Recognise how places have become the way they are and how they are changing, for examples the seaside. **History** Identify some features related to seaside holidays; recognise one or more similarities and differences between holidays now and holidays in the past. Links to QCA History Unit 3, Geography Unit 4.	**p.101: Guess how many** Use estimation skills to guess the number of sweets in a jar. Set in context of seaside game.
		Estimate, measure and compare lengths using standard units. Read a simple scale to the nearest labelled division, including using a ruler to draw and measure lines to the nearest cm.	**Science** Make and record observations and measurements. To recognise and name the parts of flowering plants. Links to QCA Science Units 2B and 2C.	**p.102: Measuring leaves** Measure the lengths and widths of leaves to the nearest cm.
		Sort shapes and describe some of their features, such as the number of sides and corners.	**ICT** Explore a variety of ICT tools. To use text and images to develop their ideas. To try things out and explore what happens. Links to QCA IT Unit 2B.	**p.103: Sorting shapes** Use a computer to create and sort shapes.
		Make and describe shapes and patterns. Recognise whole, half and quarter turns	**Art and design** Learn about visual elements including colour, pattern and shape. Links to QCA Art Unit 2C.	**p.104: Shape patterns** Print repeating patterns involving rotations of a basic shape.
7	Assess and review			**See p.116.**
8	Counting and the properties of numbers Reasoning about numbers	Understand the operation of multiplication is repeated addition or as describing an array...	**Design and technology** Investigate and evaluate a range of familiar products and structures. **Art** Explore ideas about shape and pattern; make prints based on pattern in buildings. Links with QCA Art Unit 2C.	**p.105: How many bricks?** Count the numbers of bricks in different patterns by counting in twos, fives, tens...
9	Place value, ordering, estimating Understanding + and – Mental calculation strategies (+ and –) Money and 'real-life' problems Making decisions and checking results	Know by heart doubles of all numbers to 10 and corresponding halves. Derive quickly: doubles of all numbers to at least 15 doubles of multiples of 5 to 50 halves of multiples of 10 to 100.	**Design and technology** To be taught how mechanisms (for example wheels) are used in different ways. Links to QCA D&T Unit 2A.	**p.106: Wheels** Five bicycles – how many wheels? Use wheeled vehicles to investigate doubles.
		Order whole numbers to least 100 and position them on a number line... Round numbers less than 100 to the nearest 10.	**History** Place events and objects in chronological order. Use common words and phrases relating to the passing of time. Links to QCA History Units 1 and 3.	**p.107: Old toys, new toys** Place toys from the 20th century on a 100-year time line.
		Extend understanding of the operations of addition and subtraction. Use and begin to read the related vocabulary. Use the +, – and = signs to record mental additions and subtractions in a number sentence, and recognise the use of a symbol such as ? or ? to stand for an unknown number.	**ICT** Explore a variety of ICT tools. To use text and images to develop their ideas. To try things out and explore what happens. Links to QCA IT Unit 2A.	**p.108: Calculate that! 2** Use a computer to practise addition and subtraction to 100.
10–11	Understanding × and ÷ Mental calculation strategies (× and ÷) Money and 'real-life' problems Making decisions and checking results Fractions	Order whole numbers to least 100, and position them on a number line and 100 square. Extend understanding of the operations of addition and subtraction.	**History** Use common words and phrases relating to the passing of time Study changes in their own lives of the way of life of their family and others around them. Links to QCA History Unit 1.	**p.109: Board games** Discuss and play mathematical board games.
		Use mental addition and subtraction to solve simple word problems involving numbers in real life. Explain how the problem was solved.	**Literacy** To write non-fiction texts, using texts read as models for own writing.	**p.110: Story problems** Use a word processor to write story problems involving addition and subtraction.
		Understand the operation of multiplication as repeated addition or as describing an array. Know by heart multiplication facts for the 2 and 10 times tables. Begin to know multiplication facts for the 5 times table.	**ICT** To use a variety of ICT tools. Links to QCA IT Unit 2B.	**p.111: Copy and paste** Use a computer to create arrays of stamps or other images – for example, thumbnail pictures of the children in the class. Use arrays to check multiplication facts for 2, 5 and 10 times table.
		Begin to understand division as grouping or repeated sharing.	**Geography** Identify and describe what places are like. Links to QCA Geography Unit 4.	**p.112: Fair shares** Sharing problems (division) based on a class visit to the seaside. Sharing sweets, postcards, gifts, shells, coins...
		Know by heart doubles of all numbers to 10 and corresponding halves. Derive quickly: doubles of all numbers to at least 15 doubles of multiples of 5 to 50 halves of multiples of 10 to 100..	**Design and technology** Focused practical task that develops techniques and skills. Links to QCA D&T Unit 1A.	**p.113: Doubling machine** Make 'double and half' calculators using rotating card dials.

YEAR 2

Term I	Topics	Maths objectives	Cross-curricular objectives	Activities
12–13	Measures and time, including problems Handling data	Use and begin to read vocabulary related to length and mass. Read a simple scale to the nearest labelled division, recording estimates and measurements as 'three and a bit metres long' or 'nearly 3 kilograms heavy'. Solve a given problem by sorting, classifying and organising information in a list or simple table.	**Science** Record observations and measurements. Make simple comparisons. Links to QCA Science Unit 2C. **Science** Group living things according to observable similarities and differences. Links to QCA Science Unit 2C.	**p.114: Measuring vegetables** Make length and weight measurements in the context of a champion vegetable competition. **p.115: How many legs?** Classify and sort animals by leg number.
14	Assess and review			**p.116 Assessment 1**

Term 2	Topics	Maths objectives	Cross-curricular objectives	Activities
I	Counting and properties of numbers	Read and write whole numbers to at least 100 in figures and words.	**Literacy** To read on sight high-frequency words.	**p.117: Number games** Make and play number games using numeral and number word cards.
2–4	Place value and ordering Understanding + and – Mental calculation strategies (+ and –) Money and 'real-life' problems Making decisions and checking results	Read and write whole numbers to at least 100 in figures. Compare two given two digits numbers, say which is more or less, and give a number which lies between them. Order whole numbers to at least 100. Order whole numbers to at least 100, and position them on a number line. Use and begin to read the vocabulary of estimation and approximation; give a sensible estimate of at least 50 objects.	**Geography** Recognise how places have become the way they are and how they are changing, for examples the seaside. Recognise how places compare with other places. **History** Identify some features related to seaside holidays; recognise one or more similarities and differences between holidays now and holidays in the past. Links to QCA History Unit 3, Geography Unit 4. **Literacy** To use a contents page and index to find way about text.	**p.118: Bingo!** Practise sequencing whole numbers up to 100 by making and playing a seaside Bingo game. **p.119: Find the page** Use an index to find a page number, then estimate where the page is in the book. Is it nearer the front or the back?
5–6	Measures – including problems Shape and space Reasoning about shapes	Solve mathematical problems or puzzles, recognise simple patterns and relationships, generalise and predict. Estimate, measure and compare lengths. Read a simple scale to the nearest labelled division. Use the mathematical names for common 3-D and 2-D shapes. Sort shapes and describe some of their features. Describe the symmetry of 2–D shapes. Begin to recognise line symmetry.	**History** To use common words relating to the passing of time (for example 'a long time ago'). To recognise differences between ways of life and beliefs at different times. **Science** Record observations and measurements. Recognise when a test or comparison is unfair. To find out about, and describe the movement of, familiar things. Links to QCA Science Unit 2E. **Literacy** To build collections of new words linked to particular topics. **ICT** To explore a variety of IT tools, for example word-processing software. **Science** To explore, using the sense of sight... and to record observations.	**p.120: Magic squares** Investigate simple magic number squares. **p.121: Cars on slopes** Measuring activities involving distance travelled by toy cars rolled down slopes. **p.122: Shape words** Use the computer to create a word bank of shape words. Match words to shapes. **p.123: Symmetry** Use a small mirror to investigate the symmetry of simple shapes.
7	Assess and review			See p.132.
8	Counting and the properties of numbers Reasoning about numbers	Count on in steps of 2, 3, 4, 5, 6, 10 to at least 30. Begin to know multiplication facts from the 2, 5 and 10 times tables. Use mental addition and subtraction, simple multiplication and division to solve simple word problems. Explain how the problem was solved.	**Music** To create musical patterns. To explore pulse and rhythm. Links to QCA Music Unit 4. **Literacy** To pose questions and record these in writing. **ICT** To enter and store information in a variety of forms.	**p.124: Counting beats** Count in twos, threes, fours and sixes in the context of music. **p.125: Sound puzzles** Use a cassette recorder or computer to record number puzzles for other children to answer.
9	Place value, ordering, estimating, rounding Understanding + and – Mental calculation strategies (+ and –) Money and 'real-life' problems Making decisions	Know what each digit in a two-digit number represents including zero as a place holder, and partition two digits numbers into a multiple of ten and ones (TU). Use and begin to read the vocabulary of comparing and ordering numbers, including ordinal numbers to 100. Compare to given two digits numbers, say which is more or less, and give a number that lies between them. Use known number facts and place value to add/ subtract mentally. Use known number facts and place value to carry out mentally simple multiplication and divisions.	**Design and technology** To design and construct models using construction kit components. Links to QCA Design and technology Units 1B and 1D. **Literacy** To pose questions and record these in writing. **ICT** To enter and store information in a variety of forms.	**p.126: Count the bricks** Sort and count toy bricks by grouping in tens. **p.127: Sound sums** Use a cassette recorder to record story problems involving addition, subtraction, multiplication and, division for other children to answer.
10	Understanding × and ÷ Mental calculation strategies (× and ÷) Money and 'real-life' problems Making decisions and checking results Fractions	Choose and use appropriate operations and efficient calculation strategies to solve problems. Solve simple word problems involving numbers in real-life. Begin to recognise two-digit multiples of 2, 5 or 10. Begin to recognise and find one–half and one quarter of shapes and small numbers of objects. Begin to recognise that two halves or four quarters make one whole and that two quarters and one half are equivalent.	**English** To write notes and messages. **Geography** Recognise how places compare with other places. Links to QCA Geography Unit 4. **Geography** Express their own views about people, places and environments. Links to QCA Geography Unit 4 and History Unit 3. **Design and technology** Measure, mark out, cut and shape a range of materials. Builds on QCA Unit 1C.	**p.128: School trip** Making a plan for a school trip involving costs, distance and journey times. Writing a letter to parents explaining the details of the trip. **p.129: Lucky numbers** Make and play a bran-tub game in which winning numbers are multiples of 3 or 5. **p.130: Fruit fractions** Chop fruit in halves, quarters and other fractions to make fruit salad.
11–12	Measures and time, including problems Organising and using data	Read the time to the hour, half-hour or quarter-hour on an analogue clock and a 12-hour digital clock, and understand the notation 7:30.	**History** Use common words and phrases relating to the passing of time. **Geography** Make observations about where things are located (in the local environment).	**p.131: Clocks and watches** Observe and discuss church and other clocks in the local environment.
13	Assess and review			**p.132: Assessment 2**

Planning Grid

Term 3	Topics	Maths objectives	Cross-curricular objectives	Activities
1	Counting and properties of numbers	Read and write whole numbers to at least 100 in figures and words.	**Literacy** To read on sight and spell high-frequency words.	**p.133: Numbers and words** Translating numerals to words and vice versa.
2–4	Place value and ordering Understanding + and –	Order the months of the year.	**Literacy** To read on sight high-frequency words including months of the year.	**p.134: Months and seasons** Order the months and seasons – which is the third month, which is the ninth month?
	Mental calculation strategies (+ and –) Money and 'real-life' problems	Use the vocabulary related to length and time. Measure and compare lengths and times.	**PE** Explore basic skills, actions and the ideas with increasing understanding. Describe what they have done. Travel with, send and receive a ball and other equipment in different ways.	**p.135: Measure it!** Measurements in a PE lesson.
	Making decisions and checking results	Estimate, measure and compare lengths. Recognise whole, half and quarter turns, to the left or right, clockwise or anticlockwise.	**Design and technology** To learn how mechanisms can be used in different ways. To undertake a focused practical task. Links to QCA D&T Unit 2C.	**p.136: Wind it up!** Make a wind up spider toy. Relate number of turns to distance spider rises.
5–6	Measures – including problems Shape and space Reasoning about shapes	Order whole numbers to at least 100, and position them on a number line and 100 square. Use and begin to read the vocabulary of estimation and approximation; give a sensible estimate of at least 50 objects. Read scales to the nearest labelled division.	**Science** Collect evidence by making observations and measurements. Make simple comparisons and identify simple patterns or associations.	**p.137: Make a scale** Draw and label with appropriate units a simple measuring scale on the side of a container.
		Use the mathematical names for common 3-D and 2-D shapes. Make and describe shapes.	**Design and technology** Develop ideas by putting together components. Communicate ideas using a variety of methods including making models. Links to QCA D&T Unit 1B.	**p.138: Climbing frames** Use construction kits to design different shaped climbing frames for the school playground.
7	Assess and review			**See p.146.**
8	Counting and the properties of numbers Reasoning about numbers	Order whole numbers to at least 100 and position them on a number line. Use the vocabulary of time.	**History** Study the lives of significant men, women and children drawn from the history of Britain and the wider world. Place events in chronological order. Links to QCA History Unit 4.	**p.139: The lady with the lamp** Sequence events in Florence Nightingale's life.
9	Place value, ordering, estimating Understanding + and –	Say the number names in order to at least 100, from and back to 0. Count on in twos from and back to 0... Describe and extend simple number sequences...	**History** Study past events from the history of Britain and the wider world. Links to QCA History Unit 5.	**p.140: Count the stairs** In the context of Sir Christopher Wren and St Paul's Cathedral, count/ estimate the numbers of stairs to the tops of buildings.
	Mental calculation strategies (+ and –) Money and 'real-life' problems	Solve simple mathematical problems... Use mental strategies to solve simple problems... set in real-life contexts... using doubling and halving... explaining methods and reasoning orally.	**Science** Make and record observations and measurements. Explore and describe the way some everyday materials change when they are heated.	**p.141: Making biscuits** Explore measures, doubling and halving in the context of following a recipe to make biscuits.
	Making decisions and checking results	Give instructions for moving along a route in straight lines and around right-angled corners: for example, to pass through a simple maze.	**ICT** To plan and give instructions to make things happen. To explore a variety of ICT tools. Links to QCA ICT Unit 2D. **English** To listen to retellings of traditional stories.	**p.142: Maze masters** Give directional instructions to move through a maze. Relate to the story of the Minotaur.
10–11	Understanding × and ÷ Mental calculation strategies (× and ÷)	Recognise all coins. Count on in twos, fives and tens.	**English** To participate in group discussion, making plans, investigating and sharing ideas.	**p.143: Count the coins** Use to 2p, 5p and 10p coins to count in multiples of 2, 5 and 10.
	Money and 'real-life' problems Making decisions and checking results Fractions	Begin to recognise and find one half and one quarter of shapes and small numbers of objects. Begin to recognise that two halves or four quarters make one whole and that two quarters and one half are equivalent.	**Science** Make and record observations and measurements. Make simple comparisons and identify simple patterns or associations.	**p.144: Balancing halves** Use a balance to divide sets of coins, bricks or beads in two and then in two again to find halves and quarters.
12–13	Measures and time, including problems Handling data	Solve a problem by sorting, classifying and organising information in a list or simple table.	**Music** To sing and learn songs and speak chants and rhymes.	**p.145: Top 10** Collect data to compile a Top 10 favourite songs. Present data in a table.
14	Assess and review			**p.146: Assessment 3**

1 Count the skips

Objectives

Numeracy
Say the number names in order to at least 100, from and back to zero.
Count on in twos from and back to zero or any small number, and recognise odd and even numbers to at least 30; count on in steps of 3, 4 or 5 to at least 30, from and back to zero, then from and back to any given small number.

PE
Explore basic skills, actions and ideas with increasing understanding.
Remember and repeat simple skills and actions with increasing control and co-ordination.
Links with QCA PE Games activities Unit 2.

Resources
Skipping ropes, bats and balls (or other PE apparatus that can be used for repetitive activities); a large 100 square.

Vocabulary
number
zero, one, two, three... twenty (and beyond)
zero, ten, twenty... one hundred
how many
count on
count back
count in ones, twos, threes, fours, fives...
count in tens
odd, even

Background
At the start of Year 2, most children will be counting confidently to 20 and beyond. During the year, children are expected to become familiar with all the numbers to 100, count on in ones from any small number, and start to count in twos, threes, fours, fives and tens. Counting on in intervals greater than one is an important skill for mental calculation, and supports understanding of times tables. Many activities in PE involve repetition, and counting the number of repeats supports these developing mathematical skills. It also helps to build the PE skills of timing and co-ordination.

Preparation
Prepare for a PE lesson in the hall or playground, according to your usual practice. Plan a sequence of group or paired activities involving counting and repetition – for example, skipping with a long rope, bouncing a ball, catching a ball.

Main teaching activity
Introduce the lesson by talking about repetition. *What does it mean to repeat an action? What kinds of activities in PE involve repeating an action? How do you know how many times you have repeated something?* Ask the children to perform a repeated action such as skipping, bouncing a ball or catching a ball, and to count how many times they repeat it. Ask them to try out each of the activities in turn, counting their repeats in ones (starting from zero). Children usually enjoy counting rhythmically as they perform actions. Allow some time for practice, then ask the children to choose their favourite action and count their repeats in various ways (see Differentiation).

Play a game in which you point at a starting number on the 100 square and ask the children to count on rhythmically as they perform their preferred action. Count in twos using the even numbers, then using the odd numbers. Go on to count in intervals of 3, 4 and 5.

Differentiation
More able children could experiment with counting on and back from any number in twos, threes, fours, fives and tens. Less able children should concentrate on counting on in ones, twos and tens.

Plenary
Conclude the lesson with a skipping game using a long rope turned by a child at either end, with a group of children skipping in between. Count the skips in various intervals, counting on and back, as a whole class.

Linked to
I C T

2 Make a pattern

Objectives

Numeracy

Describe and extend simple number sequences: count on in ones or tens, starting from any two-digit number; count in twos from zero or any small number, and recognise odd and even numbers to at least 30; count on in steps of 3, 4 or 5 to at least 30.

Begin to recognise two-digit multiples of 2, 5 or 10.

ICT

Plan and give instructions to make things happen.

Links to QCA ICT Units 2B and 2D.

Resources

Samples of designs based on a regular repeating motif (paintings, book covers, wallpaper, fabric, carpet); a computer with a word processing package; a blank 100 square on paper for each child.

Vocabulary

zero, one, two, three... twenty (and beyond)
zero, ten, twenty... one hundred
count in ones, twos, threes, fours, fives...
count in tens
repeating pattern
arrange
describe
odd, even
fill in

Background

Creating a regular pattern on a grid involves following a rule to generate a sequence. The same rule can be stated in different ways – for example: 'Colour every fifth square blue', 'Count four squares and colour the next one blue, repeat', 'Number the squares and colour multiples of 5 blue', 'Colour squares containing numbers that end in 0 or 5 blue'. Encouraging the children to discuss the rules they are following as they create regular patterns, and to make links between rules that produce the same result, will help them to develop the information technology skill of formulating and following rules to produce a desired result. If this activity is performed with a computer, it will also develop mouse and screen skills.

Preparation

Use a program with drawing capabilities, such as *Textease* or *Microsoft Word*, to create a 100 square on the screen for the children to colour. In *Textease*, you can simply draw a square and then 'copy and paste' it repeatedly (see page 37). If you then open the *Effects* window, the children can colour the grid squares by clicking on them individually and selecting a colour from the palette. (See illustration.) Make copies of a blank 100 square on paper; this could be

used as an alternative to the computer, or as a supplementary resource.

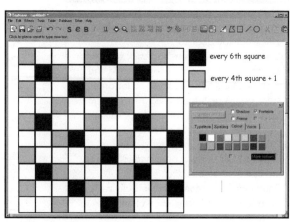

every 6th square

every 4th square + 1

Details of *Textease* are available from www.textease.com

Main teaching activity

Discuss the design samples with the whole class. Pick out the basic motifs and discuss how they have been repeated to create patterns. Demonstrate the computer activity (if appropriate) and explain how to colour squares on the grid. Let the children work in pairs to create and print a grid pattern by colouring squares at different intervals – for example, counting on in twos, fives or tens from the first square to identify and colour squares that are multiples of these numbers. Emphasise that the children should create a regular pattern by following a rule. Each pair should write down the rule they have followed for later explanation to the class. Children not working at the computer(s) can plan their designs on paper.

Differentiation

Suggest simple rules for less able children to follow. For example: 'Colour odd squares blue and even squares red'.

More able children will formulate more complex rules for themselves. For example: 'We coloured odd multiples of 5 red and even multiples blue. We coloured numbers that are not multiples of 5 green.'

Plenary

Ask the children to show their patterns to the whole class and describe the rules they followed to create them.

Linked to
I C T

3 Calculate that! 1

Objectives

Numeracy
Extend understanding of the operations of addition and subtraction.
Use and begin to read the related vocabulary.
Use the +, – and = signs to record mental additions and subtractions in a number sentence, and recognise the use of a symbol such as ? or ? to stand for an unknown number.

ICT
Explore a variety of ICT tools.
Use text and images to develop their ideas.
Try things out and explore what happens.
Links to QCA ICT Unit 2A.

Resources

A computer; a software package with text and graphic capabilities, such as *Textease* or *Microsoft Word*; a printer.

Vocabulary

add
sum
more
plus
altogether
subtract
take away
minus
equals
sign

Background

In Year 1, children should have become proficient at addition and subtraction to 10 and started to work with numbers to 20 and beyond. This computer-based activity revises and develops the children's knowledge of addition and subtraction facts. It strengthens their understanding of the symbols used in number sentences, as well as helping them to develop the ICT skills needed to drag and manipulate text and graphics on the screen.

Preparation

In advance of the lesson, prepare an on-screen document showing number sentences similar to the examples above. Black spots can be created to serve as counters by using the drawing capabilities of the software package. They can be selected and dragged around the screen by pointing and clicking the left mouse button. You can adapt the basic example as you wish for your lesson – for example, using different-coloured shapes or Clip Art of flowers, fruits or animals. Prepare a number of different pages for different groups of children (see Differentiation).

Main teaching activity

Start the lesson with some quick-fire addition and subtraction practice to 20. On the computer, show the class how to edit the text and drag the counters to complete

$$3 + 4 = 7$$

$$4 + 8 =$$

$$6 + \triangle = 9$$

each number sentence and display it in picture form (as the first problem shown above).

Ask the children to work in small groups on the problems you have prepared in advance. Each group should edit the page on screen by completing each number sentence and illustrating it with appropriate numbers of counters. When the page is completed, it can be printed. Children with good ICT skills may like to illustrate the page with their own selection of Clip Art.

Differentiation

Differentiate the difficulty of the problems worked on according to the ability of the groups. Less able children can be set problems involving the addition or subtraction of two numbers to 10, then to 20.

More able children can be challenged with problems involving the addition and subtraction of three or more numbers to 20 and beyond.

Plenary

Review the groups' printed work, reading and checking selected number sentences. Make a class display showing the children's work.

4 Days of the week

Objectives

Numeracy
Use and begin to read the vocabulary of comparing and ordering numbers, including ordinal numbers.
Use and begin to read the vocabulary related to time.
Literacy
Read on sight high-frequency words including days of the week.

Resources

Days of the week word cards (copied from photocopiable page 12). Ordinal number cards (numerals and words) from 1st and first to 7th and seventh (copied from photocopiable pages 13 and 14).

Vocabulary

days of the week
Monday, Tuesday...
weekend
first, second, third...

Background

Monday is the first day of the school week. The second day is Tuesday. *First, second, third* and so on are numbers used to label items, in this case the days of the week, in sequence or order. Numbers used in this way are called **ordinal numbers**. Children should learn to name, read and write the days of the week in sequence, and begin to use ordinal numbers to locate items in a sequence or list. This lesson is linked to word-level work in literacy on the vocabulary of time and number.

Preparation

Distribute the days of the week word cards and the ordinal number cards on desks in preparation for group work. Each group will need a full set of each type of card.

Main teaching activity

Introduce the lesson by discussing the order of the days in the week. *Which is the first day of the school week?* Hold up the appropriate pair of ordinal number cards (the word and the numeral) as you say the name of each day in the week. Discuss other examples of ordinal numbers, such as positions in a race or the order of books on a shelf. Extend the discussion by talking about the children's experiences of different days. *What is special about Saturday or Sunday? What usually happens in school on Friday?* Links could be made to RE by talking about the Biblical

creation story and the significance of a Sabbath day or day of rest. You could link this topic to history by discussing the origin of the day names: they are all derived from the names of pagan gods.

Ask the children to work in groups to sequence the day name cards and match them to the ordinal number cards. They should copy the day names and ordinal numbers into their workbooks in preparation for further written work.

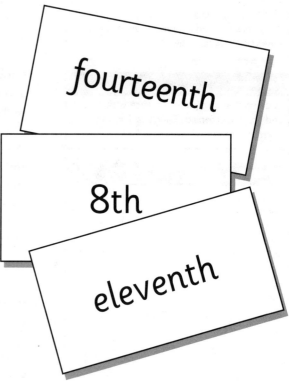

Differentiation

Less able children should concentrate on writing and sequencing the days of the week correctly.

More able children could be asked to research the origin of the day names and write a non-fiction account, or to produce some creative writing (for example, a poem) based on the days of the week.

Plenary

Review and discuss the children's written work as a class. Make a display of some children's writing about the days of the week.

Linked to
Geography
History

5 Guess how many

Objectives

Numeracy
Use and begin to read the vocabulary of estimation and approximation; give a sensible estimate of at least 50 objects.
Geography
Recognise how places have become the way they are and how they are changing.
History
Identify differences between ways of life at different times.
Links to QCA History Unit 3, and Geography Unit 4.

Resources

A tray of up to 50 beads, sweets or marbles for children to estimate; a copy of photocopiable page 147 for each child.

Vocabulary

guess how many
estimate
nearly
roughly
about the same as
close to

Background
Estimation is an advanced skill that requires practice. Do not expect children to make accurate intuitive estimates of large quantities. They may initially come up with a figure anywhere between 20 and 100 as an estimate for a group of 40 or 50. Children need considerable guidance to make sensible estimates of groups of large numbers of objects. It is not easy to estimate the number of more than 10 or so objects 'on sight' without developing strategies for subdividing the group mentally – for example, by making a rough judgement of how much space five objects take up, then 'rough counting' the number of groups of five.

'Guess my weight' and 'Guess the number of sweets in the jar' are popular fête and seaside sideshows. The activity on page 147 could be introduced in this context, or in the context of sweet shops past and present.

Preparation
Set out 20 objects on the tray, loosely grouped in fives. Distribute copies of photocopiable page 147.

Main teaching activity
Introduce the lesson by discussing 'Guess my weight' and 'Guess the number of sweets in the jar' stalls at fêtes and fairs past and present. Remind the children that **estimating** is the process of making a sensible guess how much of something there

is. Show the children the objects on the tray. Tell them that they must not count the objects one by one, but must 'estimate' roughly how many there are. *Are there 5, 10, 20, 50, 100, 1000?* Ask the children to vote on the quantity. Count the objects with the class to check their estimates. Explain the strategy of looking for smaller groups of objects to help with the estimation. Can the children see that there are four groups of about five objects? Practise estimation with further examples, including sets of up to 50 objects. When you are satisfied that the children understand what is meant by estimation, ask them to answer the questions on the photocopiable sheet.

Differentiation
Less able children should concentrate on the photocopiable sheet.

When they have completed the sheet, more able children could work in pairs to set each other estimation problems with real objects.

Plenary
Check the answers to the photocopiable sheet with the whole class, discussing the grouping strategies they used to make their estimates. The answers are: **A.** 8 **B.** 16 **C.** 30 **D.** 48. Ask the children to ask their parents and grandparents about their memories of buying sweets as children. *How were the sweets weighed? How much did they cost? What did they taste like?*

Linked to
Science

6 Measuring leaves

Objectives

Numeracy
Estimate, measure and compare lengths using standard units (m, cm).
Read a simple scale to the nearest labelled division, including using a ruler to draw and measure lines to the nearest centimetre.
Science
Make and record observations and measurements.
Recognise and name the leaf, flower, stem and root of flowering plants.
Links to QCA Science Units 2B and 2C.

Resources

Pot plants, sprouting beans, germinating cress seeds, a hyacinth bulb growing in a jar, cut flowers and/or similar examples to demonstrate the parts of a plant; a copy of photocopiable page 148 for each child; rulers labelled in 1cm divisions; pens or pencils, paper.

Vocabulary

ruler
measuring scale
centimetre
length
width
compare

Background

The ability to measure length, using standard units, is important for a mathematical understanding of measures. Measuring skills also become increasingly important in science as children start to make quantitative observations and comparisons during their investigations and experiments. In this activity, the children identify leaves and other parts of a plant, then use a ruler to measure the widths and lengths of a variety of leaves. The lesson could be developed into an extended science investigation in which the children collect, identify and measure leaves from the local environment.

Preparation

Set out the copies of page 148, rulers, pencils and paper on tables in advance of the lesson. Set out the plants for demonstration around the classroom.

Main teaching activity

Introduce the lesson by showing the children a centimetre ruler and discussing how it is used. Discuss the terms 'length' and 'width'. Make measurements of the lengths or widths of some items around the classroom, such as pencils, hands and books. Show the children

how to record their measurements, writing both the quantity measured and the measurement unit. For example: 'Pencil length = 14cm'.

Show the children the various plants around the classroom, and identify the roots, stems, leaves and flowers together. Talk about the different shapes and textures of the leaves: *Which leaves are pointed? Which are rounded? Which have rough edges? Which have smooth edges?*

Show the children the photocopiable sheet and ask them to measure and record the lengths and widths of the different leaves.

Differentiation

The children can develop the activity by collecting leaves from trees in the school grounds to measure. Less able children could sort these leaves by size.

More able children could make more detailed comparisons, such as:
● *Are all the leaves from the same tree the same size?*
● *Which tree has the longest leaves?*
● *Which tree has the broadest leaves?*

Plenary

Review the children's measurements of the leaves on the photocopiable sheet. Make sure that all the children can measure with a ruler to the nearest centimetre. In a follow-up science lesson, create a class display of the children's investigations of leaves they have collected.

Linked to
I C T

7 Sorting shapes

Background

Geometrical shapes can be readily created on a computer screen with the drawing tools in word-processing and design packages such as *Textease* and *Microsoft Word*. In *Word*, for example, select the *Toolbars* item from the *View* menu and check 'Drawing' so that the toolbar is displayed. Click on *AutoShapes* and select *Basic Shapes* to draw triangles, squares, rectangles, pentagons, hexagons, octagons and other shapes. Children can develop their ICT skills, along with their knowledge of shapes and shape vocabulary, by creating designs and patterns with shapes drawn in this way.

Preparation

In advance of the lesson, check that you can use your chosen program confidently to create shapes and move them around the screen.

Main teaching activity

Introduce the lesson by discussing the properties of various cut-out shapes and sorting them according to the number of sides and angles. Explain that the children are going to create and sort shapes on the computer.

Demonstrate how to draw basic shapes with the computer package and drag them around the screen. You could also demonstrate how to change the colour of the 'border' and 'fill'. Set the children the task of working in pairs or small groups to create a shape-sorting puzzle on the screen. They

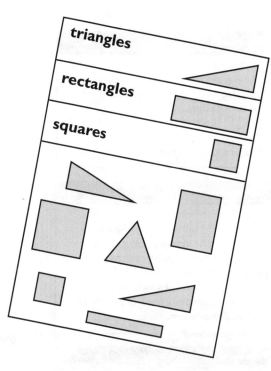

should draw lines to divide a page into three or more regions, label each region except the bottom one with a category of shape (such as 'triangles' or 'squares'), and then create a number of shapes for sorting in the bottom region of the page. An example is shown above. The groups can then challenge each other to sort the shapes into the correct categories by dragging and dropping, then print the completed page.

Differentiation

Less able children could concentrate on three types of basic shape – for example, circles, triangles and rectangles.

More able children could create more complex shape-sorting sheets.

Plenary

Review the children's printouts as a class. Check that all the shapes have been sorted correctly, and create a class display of the children's work.

8 Shape patterns

Objectives

Numeracy
Make and describe shapes and patterns.
Recognise whole, half and quarter turns.
Art and design
Be taught about visual elements, including colour, pattern and shape.
Links to QCA Art Unit 2C.

Resources

Materials for printing basic shapes (the children could cut shapes from potatoes, or use commercial sponge printing shapes); paper, trays of liquid paint, newspaper, cleaning materials; examples of designs based on repetition of simple shapes or motifs (for example, a book of paintings by MC Escher); safety mirrors.

Vocabulary

shape
pattern
repeat
rotate
turn

Background

Repeated patterns printed from basic shapes are a common feature of decorative design in buildings, fabrics and wallpapers. Exploring the patterns created by rotation and repetition of a simple shape, for example a rectangle or a T, introduces both the vocabulary of turning and ideas about symmetry. This activity also develops the children's awareness of pattern, shape and colour in the context of art and design.

Preparation

Cover the tables and set out the printing materials according to your normal practice for a paint-based art lesson.

Main teaching activity

Show and discuss some examples of designs based on repetition of simple shapes. Demonstrate how a shape can be printed, then rotated (or repositioned) and printed again to produce a motif for a repetitive design.

● This example is based on rotation and repetition of a simple T shape:

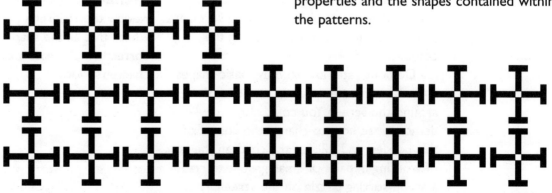

● This example has been created with a triangle:

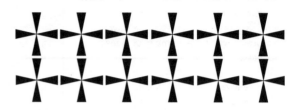

As you create a pattern, use the vocabulary of turning to describe the process: *a quarter turn to the right, a half turn, three-quarters of a turn* and so on. Introduce some ideas about symmetry: *Does the pattern look the same if it is turned upside down? Does the pattern look the same if it is reflected in a mirror?* (The children could check for mirror symmetry using safety mirrors.) Identify other shapes that appear in the patterns – for example, the four-pointed white stars in the pattern above.

Ask the children to choose a basic shape with which to create their pattern. Let them experiment with different combinations of colour, rotation and position before they finally select a motif to create a repeating design.

Differentiation

Children's work will be differentiated by the complexity of their designs and the skill with which they create them. More able children could experiment with designs based on combinations of two or more shapes.

Plenary

Look at and talk about the children's designs. Identify their basic motifs, their symmetry properties and the shapes contained within the patterns.

Linked to
D & T
Art & design

9 How many bricks?

Objectives

Numeracy
Understand the operation of multiplication as repeated addition or as describing an array.
Design and technology
Investigate and evaluate a range of familiar products.
Art
Be taught about visual elements, including pattern and shape.
Links with QCA Art Unit 2C.

Resources

A copy of photocopiable page 149 for each child; samples of other items arranged in regular arrays – for example: stamps on a sheet, biscuits on a tray, a wall made from toy bricks, playing cards laid out in a regular pattern.

Vocabulary

zero, one, two, three... twenty (and beyond)
zero, ten, twenty... one hundred
zero, one hundred, two hundred... one thousand
count in ones, twos, threes, fours, fives...
tens
pattern
repeat

Background

This activity develops counting and estimation skills, and prepares children for work on times tables and multiplication. When they are first asked to count the number of bricks in a wall or similar array of objects, children will count each brick individually. Recognising that objects can be grouped in twos, fives, tens and so on greatly increases the efficiency of counting. Opportunities for grouping and counting in this way may arise in various contexts – for example, counting stamps on a sheet, eggs in a box or tiles on a wall. Repetition of basic units is a feature of the design of many buildings and other artefacts. This work is thus linked to observation and experiment in design, technology and art.

Preparation

Distribute copies of page 149 and collect arrays of items for demonstration. Set out some arrays of playing cards or similar objects for counting, as shown in the illustration.

Main teaching activity

Demonstrate a few structures in which shapes are arranged in an ordered way – for example, a wall of toy bricks. Ask the children to suggest other situations where objects are arranged regularly. Paving slabs in the street, squares in a bar of chocolate and stickers on a sheet are all examples.

Playing card arrays

Show the children the arrays of cards (or similar items) and ask them to count the cards. Ask: *Is there a more efficient way of counting the cards?* Explain that a 2 × 4 array could be counted in twos, and a 3 × 5 array in fives. Count the arrays in this way with the whole class, then check your answers by counting the cards one at a time. Ask the children to work with a partner to count the bricks on the photocopiable sheet. They should count the arrays using the intervals suggested, then experiment with counting in different ways. Which is the 'quickest' way of counting each set of bricks?

Differentiation

Set out some more complex arrays of cards to challenge the more able children's counting skills, for example 7 × 11 or 6 × 13.
Less able children should concentrate on counting simple arrays based on twos, fives and tens.

Plenary

Reinforce the children's counting skills at the end of the lesson by counting the arrays on page 149 and those you have set out around the class together, using appropriate groups for counting. Ask individuals to set out regular card arrays for others to count.

Linked to
D & T

10 Wheels

Objectives

Numeracy
Know by heart doubles of all numbers to 10 and the corresponding halves.
Derive quickly: doubles of all numbers to at least 15; doubles of multiples of 5 to 50; halves of multiples of 10 to 100.
Design and technology
Be taught how mechanisms can be used in different ways (for example, wheels).
Links to QCA D&T Unit 2A Vehicles.

Resources

A copy of photocopiable page 150 for each child; a selection of wheeled toy vehicles.

Vocabulary

double
half, halve
altogether
count
how many?

Background
Doubling and halving are important calculation skills. Children in Year 2/ Scottish Primary 3 should know the doubles of all numbers to 10 by heart. They can use this knowledge to recognise the patterns created by doubling and halving, and thus to derive quickly the doubles and halves of larger numbers. They should eventually be able to explain, for example, that doubling any number ending in 3 produces a number ending in 6 because double 3 equals 6.

Doubling and halving exercises can be set in a counting context, such as counting the number of wheels on a number of bicycles. Each bicycle has two wheels, so the number of wheels is double the number of bicycles. This activity links doubling and halving to work on wheels and wheeled vehicles in the context of technology.

Preparation
Distribute copies of page 150 on tables in advance of the lesson.

Main teaching activity
Introduce the lesson by looking at toy vehicles and counting their wheels. Ask: *Which vehicles have two wheels? Which vehicles have four wheels? Are there any vehicles with three wheels or more than four wheels?* Discuss the advantages and disadvantages of having certain numbers of wheels. For example, bicycles are light and fast, but not very stable until you have learned to balance! Having

four wheels makes a vehicle more stable, but can make turning sharp corners more difficult. Use the toy vehicles as the basis for some simple problems: *How many wheels are there altogether on two cars? How many wheels are there altogether on three bicycles?*

Discuss how to calculate the number of wheels on several bicycles by doubling the number of bicycles. Introduce the reverse process of halving: the number of bicycles is half the number of wheels. The number of wheels on several cars can be calculated by doubling and then doubling again.

Ask the children to work individually to complete the photocopiable sheet.

Differentiation
Less able children should concentrate on completing the first table on page 150, which involves doubles to 10.

More able children should proceed to complete the second, third and fourth tables, which extend the activity to doubles of integers to 20, doubles of multiples of 5 to 50, and halves of multiples of 10 to 100.

Plenary
Look together at a completed copy of page 150. Discuss the number patterns in the tables. Conclude the lesson with some quick-fire doubling and halving questions.

11 Old toys, new toys

Objectives

Numeracy
Order whole numbers to least 100 and position them on a number line.
History
Place events and objects in chronological order.
Use common words and phrases relating to the passing of time.

Resources

A 0–100 number line labelled in tens; a 0–100 number line with the positions of tens marked but not labelled; copies of photocopiable page 151; some toys (or pictures of toys) from different decades of the twentieth century.

Vocabulary

year
century
decade
estimate
just over
just under
close to
order
before
after
between
halfway

Background
Estimating the positions of numbers on an unlabelled number line requires children to subdivide the length of the line mentally. Like estimating quantities of 50 or more, this is a difficult skill that requires considerable practice. The context of an 'age' line running from 0 to 100 years, with toys or other objects being placed along it, provides a useful link to work in history on timelines, the sequence of events, and changes between the past and the present.

Preparation
Display the number lines in preparation for whole-class discussion. Make a copy of page 151 for each child.

Main teaching activity
Begin the lesson by discussing the position of numbers on the 0–100 number line with the whole class. Demonstrate that 50 is halfway between 0 and 100, 10 is close to zero, 80 is close to 100 but not as close as 90, and so on. Now look at an unlabelled number line. Ask individual children to come out and point to the positions of different numbers. Discuss their accuracy with the whole class.

Now consider the toy timeline on page 151. Explain that it runs from zero years old to 100 years old. The divisions mark intervals of ten years. Explain that a ten-year period is called a 'decade', and that we name each decade by the 'tens' number it contains (for example, the years 1990–9 were called 'the nineties'). Hold up various toys (or pictures of toys); say which decade each toy came from, and ask a child to position it on the timeline. The children should then complete the photocopiable sheet, drawing an arrow to connect each toy to its age on the timeline.

Differentiation
Less able children should concentrate on positioning the toys within the correct decade.

Challenge more able children to estimate the position of each toy more accurately on the timeline. The line is 20cm long, so each year is represented by 2mm.

Plenary
Review the ages of the toys or pictures you have provided, and their locations on the timeline, with the whole class. Follow up by locating some significant twentieth-century events on the line, such as the end of the Second World War and the landing of the first human being on the Moon.

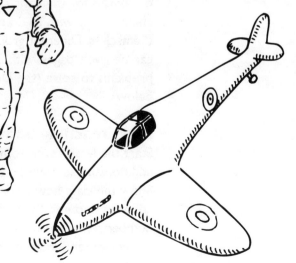

12 Calculate that! 2

Objectives

Numeracy
Extend understanding of the operations of addition and subtraction.

Use and begin to read the related vocabulary.

Use the +, – and = signs to record mental additions and subtractions in a number sentence, and recognise the use of a symbol such as □ or △ to stand for an unknown number.

ICT
Explore a variety of ICT tools.

Use text and images to develop their ideas.

Try things out and explore what happens.

Links to QCA ICT Unit 2A.

Resources

A computer running a software package with text and graphic capabilities, such as *Textease* or *Microsoft Word*; a printer.

Vocabulary

add
sum
more
plus
altogether
subtract
take away
minus
equals
sign

Background
This lesson builds on Lesson 3. It extends the computer-based number sentence activity introduced in that lesson to addition and subtraction problems to 100, and develops the children's ICT skills in manipulating text and graphics.

Preparation
Prepare an on-screen document similar to the example shown. In this example, the counters have been arranged in tens and ones. A group of ten counters can be created by 'copying and pasting' a single counter, selecting the whole group and then 'grouping' the selection using the appropriate option from the *Draw* menu. As was suggested in Lesson 3, this basic design can be adapted by substituting different-coloured shapes, flowers, fruit or animals for the basic counters. The children may wish to do this for themselves. Different groups of children can be given 'pages' with different problems to solve (see Differentiation below).

Main teaching activity
Start the lesson with some quick-fire addition and subtraction practice to 100. Show the class how to drag the counters and edit the text in the number sentences to solve problems on the computer screen, in the way that the first problem has been completed in the example shown below.

According to the number of computers available, set the children to work in small groups on the problems you have prepared in advance. Each group should arrange and edit the page on-screen so that all the number sentences are complete and illustrated by appropriate numbers of counters. The completed pages can be printed.

Differentiation
The difficulty of the problems prepared in advance can be differentiated according to the ability of the groups. Less able children could be set problems involving the addition or subtraction of two numbers to 20 and then to 100.

More able children could be challenged with problems involving the addition and subtraction of three or more numbers to 100 and beyond.

Plenary
Review the groups' printed work, reading and checking some of their number sentences. Make a class display of the children's work.

$$15 + 6 \ = \ 21$$

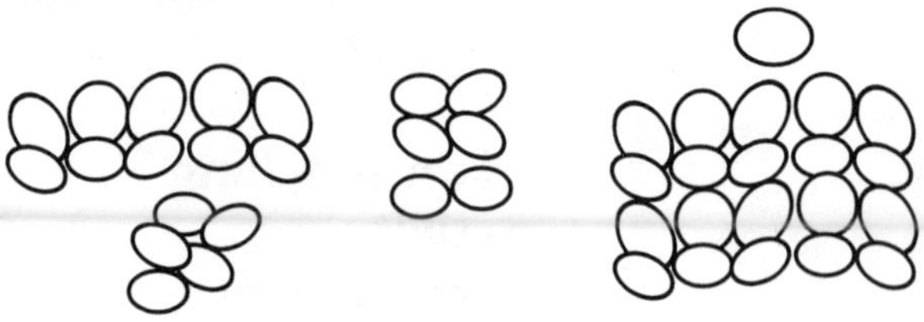

$$24 + 8 \ =$$

$$14 + \triangle \ = \ 30$$

Linked to
H i s t o r y

13 Board games

Objectives

Numeracy
Order whole numbers to least 100,
and position them on a number line and
100 square.
Extend understanding of the operations
of addition and subtraction.

History
Use common words and phrases relating
to the passing of time.
Study changes in their own lives and the
way of life of their family or others
around them.
Links to QCA History Unit 1.

Resources

Copies of photocopiable pages 152 and 153,
dice, shakers, counters; a collection of old
board games (if available); a 0–100 number
line.

Vocabulary

count on
count back
subtract
score
double
row
column
dice
counters

Background

Through playing
simple board games
such as Snakes and
Ladders, children
practise a range of
number skills:
sequencing, number
comparison, addition
and subtraction.
Children's board
games have been
popular since
Victorian times and
before, and many
families will have 'old'
games stored away in
the loft that children
can play with their
siblings and other
family members.
Making a collection of
old games and locating
them on a timeline
links this topic to
work in history
where the children
investigate ways in
which their
family's life has
changed.

do you have to do when you play this game?
'You have to count on each time you throw
the dice, or add the number on the dice to
the number on your square, to know where
to go next...'

Ask the children to play the two games
on the photocopiable sheets in pairs or
small groups. Game 1 involves numbers to
20 and should be suitable for all the children.
Game 2 involves more difficult number
operations with numbers up to 100.

Differentiation

Less able children can concentrate on
playing game 1.

More able children can play game 2. They
might go on to devise and make their own
simple board games.

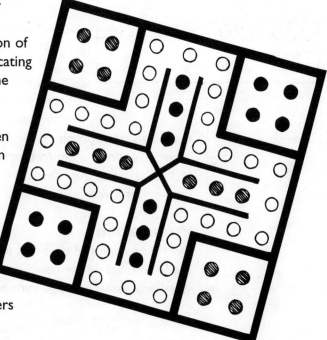

Preparation

Make a copy of each photocopiable
game sheet for each child. Set out
the sheets with dice, shakers and counters
on the tables.

Main teaching activity

Introduce the lesson by looking at some
examples of old board games with the class.
Encourage the children to judge the age of
each game from its condition and the style of
its pieces and packaging. *Is it nearly new, a few
years old or very old?* Look for specific
evidence of its age, such as a publication date
in the rule book. Discuss the object of the
game and its rules, placing particular
emphasis on the maths involved. *What sums*

Plenary

Conclude the lesson with a discussion of
board games. Which board games do the
children prefer? Do they like games that
depend on luck, such as Snakes and Ladders,
or games where they have to think ahead,
such as dominoes and draughts? Suggest that
the children interview their parents or
grandparents about board games they played
as children.

14 Story problems

Objectives

Numeracy
Use mental addition and subtraction to solve simple word problems involving numbers in 'real life'. Explain how the problem was solved.
Literacy
Write non-fiction texts, using texts read as models for own writing.
ICT
Explore a variety of ICT tools.

Resources

A copy of photocopiable page 154 for each child; a computer and word-processing software; a printer; a board or flip chart.

Vocabulary

addition
subtraction
word problems
add
plus
minus
subtract

Background

Solving mathematical problems in real life involves mentally translating an event or relationship expressed in words into a calculation. To develop this skill, children need to tackle a variety of problems expressed in real-life contexts – for example, *There were eighteen people on the bus and six got off. How many were left?* As children become familiar with this type of problem, they should be able to summarise the necessary calculation: '18 take away 6'. In this activity, the children use a word-processor to write their own story problems for their friends to solve. This allows them to practise literacy and ICT skills as they develop their mathematical reasoning.

Preparation

Distribute copies of page 154 in advance of the lesson. Set up the computer(s) with the word-processing package running.

Main teaching activity

Introduce the lesson by looking at the sample problems on the photocopiable sheet. Discuss each problem and ask the children to identify the calculation they need to make in order to solve it. Write each number sentence on the board. Try to express the calculations in alternative (but equivalent) vocabulary during the discussion. For example: *18 take away 6, 18 minus 6, 6 from 18, 18 subtract 6...*

Explain that the children's task is to write their own similar word problems for the rest of the class to solve. Suggest that they start by using the problems set out on the photocopiable sheet, but substitute alternative names, animals or items. They may wish to choose a theme for their problems, such as pets or football games. Ask the children to work in groups at the computer(s), discussing and writing their story problems. If insufficient computers are available, some groups could work with pencil and paper.

Differentiation

Less able children should concentrate on producing their own single-step versions of problems 1–3 on page 154.

More able children could develop a theme and produce problems involving two or more steps.

Plenary

Ask representatives of the groups to read out some of the problems they have written. Solve these problems as a class, writing each number sentence on the board.

The answers are: **1.** 13 **2.** 15 **3.** 8 **4.** 9 **5.** 8 **6.** 5 **7.** 11 **8.** 18 **9.** 6 **10.** 13

15 Copy and paste

Objectives

Numeracy
Understand the operation of multiplication as repeated addition or as describing an array.
Know by heart multiplication facts for the 2 and 10 times tables.
Begin to know multiplication facts for the 5 times table.
ICT
Use a variety of ICT tools.
Links to QCA ICT Unit 2B: Creating pictures.

Resources

A computer running software with drawing facilities, such as *Microsoft Word* or *Textease*; samples of Clip Art or thumbnail pictures, perhaps produced by the children with a digital camera.

Vocabulary

multiply
lots of
groups of
times
array
row, column

Background
Multiplication of whole numbers is clearly illustrated by rectangular arrays. For example, the multiplication of 2 and 5 can be represented by a 2 × 5 array of objects as shown below. Such arrays are readily created on the computer. A thumbnail picture or item of clip art can be copied and pasted repeatedly to produce an array. Drawing software usually includes commands for aligning and distributing objects to produce a regular pattern. Using the computer to produce rectangular arrays forms the basis of a numeracy lesson that also helps to develop important ICT skills.

Preparation
Check that you can use your chosen software to form arrays by 'copying and pasting' images. Print some sample arrays (using groups of 2, 5 and 10) with which to introduce the lesson.

Main teaching activity
Start the lesson by using arrays similar to the one shown below to link counting in twos, fives and tens to multiplication. Discuss examples of pictures and objects that are arranged in arrays: stamps on a sheet, eggs in a tray, squares of chocolate in a bar and so on.

Explain that the children are going to create their own arrays of pictures or photographs on the computer. Demonstrate how to select, copy and paste an image to create an array. Write a list of array dimensions on the board for children to reproduce (for example: 2 × 4, 3 × 5, 7 × 5, 6 × 10 and so on).

The children should work in small groups at the computer(s) to create their arrays. Ask them to label each array with the multiplication fact to which it corresponds (for example: 7 × 5 = 35).

Differentiation
Less able children should concentrate on creating small arrays to illustrate multiplication facts from the 2 and 5 times tables.

More able children could extend the activity to larger arrays, illustrating more complex multiplication facts (for example, doubles of numbers to 15, multiples of 4, multiples of 6).

Plenary
With the class, look at printouts of the children's arrays. Use them to check the multiplication facts they illustrate.

2 × 5 = 10

16 Fair shares

Objectives

Numeracy
Begin to understand division as grouping (repeated subtraction) or sharing.
Geography
Identify and describe what places are like.
Links to QCA Geography Unit 4: Going to the seaside.

Resources

Collections of small items with a seaside theme, for example shells, pebbles, postcards, sweets, novelties; a copy of photocopiable page 155 for each child.

Vocabulary

divide
share
share equally
equal groups
one each, two each, three each...

Background

The idea of sharing sweets, pencils or beads fairly is one possible basis for an initial understanding of division. If 6 sweets are shared between 2 people, each person receives 3 sweets – so 6 divided by 2 equals 3. This activity is a simple sharing exercise based on items found at the seaside. It is thus linked to work in geography on seaside visits and describing the characteristics of a location.

Preparation

Sort out the items for sharing, and distribute the copies of page 155 on tables, in advance of the lesson.

Main teaching activity

Introduce the lesson by showing the class the seaside collections. Ask: *Where do you think these items are from? What is it like at the seaside? Where at the seaside would you find these things?* Ask the children about their own experiences of seaside holidays. *At what time of year do people generally go to the seaside? What seaside resorts have you visited? What shops did you find at the seaside? How were these different from the shops in your high street? Did you bring home any souvenirs? What things did you find on the beach?*

Explain that you want to share out the various items fairly between pairs of children. Choose a pair of children and

share a group of up to 20 items between them. Repeat with other pairs of children and groups of items. Introduce the vocabulary of division (for example, *12 divided by 2 equals 6*) and write the corresponding number sentence on the board (*12 ÷ 2 = 6*).

Ask the children to work independently on the photocopiable sheet, completing each diagram and number sentence as in the first example.

Differentiation

Less able children may need to use real objects to help them solve the division problems.

Challenge more able children to create some division problems of their own, with a seaside theme, on another sheet of paper.

Plenary

Review the answers to the photocopiable sheet with the whole class. Conclude with some quick-fire division problems, such as *8 divided by 2* and *10 divided by 2*.

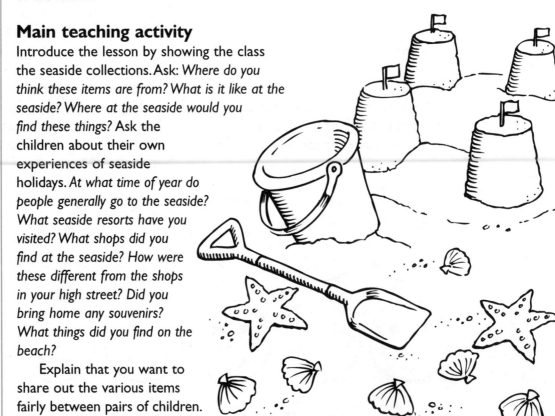

17 Doubling machine

Objectives

Numeracy
Know by heart doubles of all numbers to 10 and the corresponding halves.
Design and technology
Carry out focused practical tasks that develop techniques and skills.
Links to QCA D&T Unit 1A: Moving pictures.

Resources

A copy of photocopiable page 156 for each child; card, scissors, rulers, pencils, card punches, paper fasteners.

Vocabulary

double
half
halve

Background

Knowledge by heart of doubles, halves and other number facts is an important aid to mental calculation. In this activity, the children use design and technology skills to make a simple card 'doubling machine'. The machine consists of a circular card number dial turned by a lever. Each number from 1 to 10 and its double are displayed in cut-out windows. Making and using the machine will reinforce the children's knowledge of the number bonds the machine displays.

Preparation

Distribute copies of page 156 in advance of the lesson. Set out the technology materials on tables, according to your usual practice for a practical lesson. Normal safety practice for working with scissors and other practical equipment must be followed. Make a sample calculating machine to demonstrate to the class.

Main teaching activity

Introduce the lesson with some doubling and halving practice. Do the children know the double of every number to 10? Do they know the corresponding halves? Test their knowledge with some quick-fire questions: *double five, double three, half twelve, half eighteen, double eight* and so on.

Develop the lesson by demonstrating the sample machine to the children. Show how numbers and their doubles appear in the cut-out windows as the lever arm is turned. Read through the instructions on the photocopiable sheet with the children, and discuss the steps they need to take in order

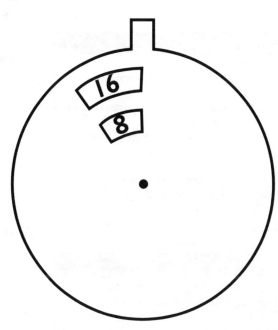

to complete their machine. They need to fill in each number and its double in the spaces in the number rings, so that the numbers appear correctly in the windows as the parts of the machine are rotated. Some children may need adult help to cut out and assemble the parts.

Differentiation

Most children should make the basic doubling machine.

Suggest that more able children produce alternative versions of the machine to show doubles of numbers to 50. They could also adapt the basic machine for use with other number facts – for example, halves or times tables.

Plenary

Ask selected children to demonstrate their machines to the class, showing how they dial a number and read off its double. Conclude the lesson with some quick-fire doubling and halving problems.

Linked to
S c i e n c e

18 Measuring vegetables

Background

In Year 2, children should start to measure using standard units. They should read scales to the nearest labelled division and record readings in their own words. They should note when a reading is 'a bit more than' or 'not quite' equal to a whole number of units – for example, 'just over 2kg'. The measurement activities on photocopiable page 157 are based on a vegetable competition, and are thus linked to science work on the identification of plants and their parts.

Preparation

Set out a display of vegetables, rulers and weighing scales in preparation for a class demonstration. Distribute copies of page 157 on the tables in advance of the lesson.

Main teaching activity

Introduce the lesson by identifying and comparing the different vegetables. Discuss which part of the plant each vegetable comes from. For example, carrots are roots (and potatoes are root growths); leeks are stems; pumpkins and tomatoes are fruits; peas and beans are seeds (and runner beans are seed pods); cabbages and broccoli are made up of leaves.

Demonstrate how to measure and record the mass and the length of selected vegetables, writing each measurement to the nearest whole number on a card. Display the vegetables with their cards, and ask the

children to pick out 'the longest runner bean' or 'the heaviest potato'.

Ask the children to work individually, using rulers, to complete the photocopiable sheet. They should measure each carrot to the nearest centimetre, write the measurement on the carrot, and draw lines linking the appropriate carrots to the prizes. Similarly, they should record the weight of each pumpkin to the nearest kilogram (as indicated by the scales) and award the prizes appropriately.

Differentiation

Less able children should be encouraged to record their measurements to the nearest whole number.

More able children should include phrases such as 'nearly', 'a bit more than' or 'not quite'. Children who complete the activity on the photocopiable sheet quickly could weigh and measure some actual vegetables.

Plenary

Review the answers to the photocopiable sheet and identify the champion vegetables. This lesson could be followed up by running a simple vegetable-growing competition in the class – for example, to grow the tallest bean plant or the longest carrot. Beans or carrot seeds could be planted in pots filled with 'grow bag' soil and placed on a sunny windowsill.

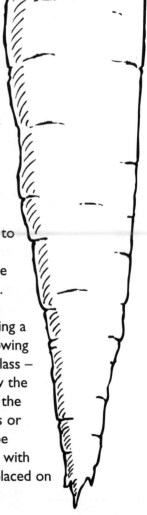

19 How many legs?

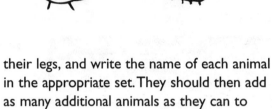

Objectives

Numeracy
Solve a given problem by sorting, classifying and organising information in a list or simple table.

Science
Group living things according to observable similarities and differences.

Links to QCA Science Unit 2C: Variation.

Resources

A copy of photocopiable page 158 for each child; pictures or photographs of a variety of animals with different numbers of legs: fish, birds, mammals, insects and so on.

Vocabulary

table
group
list
sort
column

Background
The ability to collect and organise data is an important mathematical skill. It is also an important investigative skill in other areas of the curriculum, particularly in science. In this activity, the children sort animals by number of legs. The activity links to work in science on comparing different living things and identifying similarities and differences between them.

Preparation
Cut out suitable pictures or photographs from magazines. Distribute copies of page 158 in advance of the lesson.

Main teaching activity
Introduce the lesson by looking at some pictures of animals and counting their legs. Can the children give you examples of animals with two legs, four legs, six legs, eight legs, more than eight legs, no legs? Discuss categories of animals:
● *What kind of animals have six legs?* (insects)
● *What kind of animals have four legs?* (mammals, reptiles or amphibians)
● *Does only one kind of animal have two legs?* (No: birds and humans have two legs.)
    The children should identify the animals shown on the photocopiable sheet, count

their legs, and write the name of each animal in the appropriate set. They should then add as many additional animals as they can to each set (including drawings if they wish).

Differentiation
Less able children should concentrate on identifying and sorting the animals shown on the photocopiable sheet.
    More able children can be challenged to write at least six animal names in each set – who can write the most?

Plenary
Review the children's sets as a class. Look for patterns. Have the children noticed that there are no animals with odd numbers of legs? Discuss the fact that nearly all animals have **symmetrical** bodies whose right and left sides are mirror images. This means that they generally have an even number of legs, wings and other limbs. *Can you think of an exception? (Starfish have five legs.)*

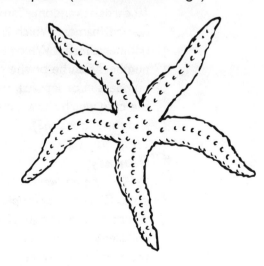

20 Assessment 1

Objectives

The assessment activities in this book are designed to introduce Key Stage 1 children to SAT-style questions. They are set in cross-curricular contexts based on the preceding term's lessons. The questions in Assessment 1 test children's progress in: recognising odd numbers and multiples of 2; measuring lengths; and solving 'story problems' involving addition and subtraction.

Resources

Copies of photocopiable page 159, pencils; a pack of number cards to 100.

Preparation

Make copies of the assessment sheet in advance of the lesson. If you feel that the sheet is too 'busy', the questions could be separated and enlarged on individual sheets.

Lesson introduction

Begin the assessment lesson by reviewing the relevant cross-curricular topics covered during the term. Remind children of some of the projects and investigations they have undertaken, and ask them to recall and recount their work. Emphasise the mathematical content – for example:
Do you remember how we measured the length and widths of the leaves to the nearest centimetre?

Main assessment activity

Distribute the sheets and set the children to work on them individually. Guide the whole class through the questions one at a time, reading the text with them, and prompting them to formulate and fill in their answers. Try to make the whole activity enjoyable!

Practical activity

Shuffle the cards and ask the child to select 10 cards at random. Can the child say the number names? Which is the smallest number chosen? Which is the largest number? Can he or she place the selected numbers in order? Ask the child to point to the card which shows, for example, six tens and three ones (63).

Plenary

Review the answers to the questions as a class. Collect the completed question sheets to use as an aid to judging individual children's progress, and to include in your records. The answers are shown on the right.

1	2	3	4	5
6	7	8	9	10
11	12	13	14	15
16	17	18	19	20
21	22	23	24	25

1	2	3	4	5
6	7	8	9	10
11	12	13	14	15
16	17	18	19	20
21	22	23	24	25

Leaf 1 length = 7cm, width = 5cm
Leaf 2 length = 10cm, width = 3cm

$18 + 9 = 27$
$30 - 20 + 6 = 16$

21 Number games

Objectives

Numeracy
Read whole numbers to at least 100 in figures and words.
Begin to recognise two-digit multiples of 5 or 10.
Literacy
Read on sight high-frequency words.

Resources

Packs of number cards showing the numbers 0–100 as numerals and (separately) as words. These are available commercially, or they could be made from photocopiable resource pages 8–11 by copying, backing with card and cutting out.

Vocabulary

number
zero, one, two, three... twenty (and beyond)
even
odd
multiple
equal

Background

This lesson provides work on the numerals and number words to 100, building on work in Year 1 (Lessons 1 and 27) to help the children develop sight recognition of number symbols and words and begin to recognise odd numbers, even numbers, doubles of numbers, and multiples of 5 and 10.

Preparation

Prepare the number cards, sorting them into sets of mixed word and numeral cards appropriate for the games you plan to play – for example, cards 0–20, multiples of 10, multiples of 5, cards 0–100 and so on.

Main teaching activity

Introduce the lesson by using the cards as flash cards. After the children have spent some minutes practising sight-reading the number names, play some games. For example, the children could:
● raise their hands for even numbers but not for odd numbers
● call out 'multiple 5' or 'multiple 10' when a multiple of 5 or 10 is displayed

● divide the pack in two, with two children displaying cards simultaneously to the class, who call out 'Snap' if the cards are both even or both odd
● play Snap with multiples
● call out 'Double Snap' if an equivalent numeral and number word appear together.

Divide the class into groups to play the games with subsets of the cards, as appropriate to their ability levels (see Differentiation).

Differentiation

Less able children could play simple Snap games with limited card sets (for example, only the numbers 0–20).

Challenge more able children to devise number games of their own, using all the cards.

Plenary

Use the plenary session to sort the cards back into the original sets. Distribute the jumbled cards between the children, then collect the number word cards and numeral cards in sequence. The children should look at their cards and hand you the numbers they hold as you call them out.

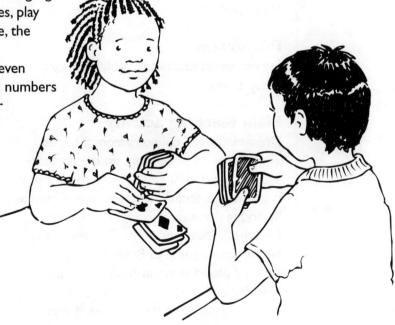

Linked to
H i s t o r y

22 Bingo!

Background

When playing Bingo, children have to connect the number words they hear to the numerals displayed on their cards. The numbers on each card are organised in columns according to their size. As the children search to see whether they have the numbers called, they will get used to the number groupings in tens and develop a feel for their relative positions. Most children will soon discover that they do not need to look at all the numbers on the card, but only to check the appropriate tens column. The topic is linked to history through discussion of where and how Bingo has been played in the past. Bingo has been a popular game since Victorian times (when it was known as Housey-Housey).

Preparation

Set out the resources on tables for each group to use.

Main teaching activity

Draw numbered counters from a bag and ask children to place them on the correct squares of a 1–100 grid. Demonstrate that it is possible to find the correct square rapidly by noting that successive rows are tens, twenties, thirties and so on. Talk about the history of the game of Bingo. Have the children played Bingo at home or at the seaside? Explain that it was a popular 'parlour' game in Victorian times. It was also popular among the passengers on transatlantic liners such as the Titanic.

Explain that the children are going to make and play their own Bingo games. They should work in groups to make Bingo cards, counters and blank card squares (30 for each Bingo card). The Bingo cards can be cut from copies of page 160 and backed with card; a copy of the 1–100 grid can be cut up to make the counters, and another used as the caller's grid.

Each group now plays the game, taking turns to be the caller. As the numbers are drawn and called, the players cover them on their cards with blank card squares. Prompt the children with questions such as *How many more numbers do you need?* and *Who has got the most numbers so far?* as the games proceed. The caller places the drawn numbers in the correct squares on the 1–100 grid. The first player to cover all of his or her numbers calls out 'Bingo!' to win.

Differentiation

Less able children should play with one Bingo card.

More able children can use two or three Bingo cards simultaneously.

Plenary

Talk about other number games the children have played or are aware of, such as raffles, lotteries and tombolas. Ask: *Where have you played this? Have your family played it? How is it similar to Bingo? How is it different?*

23 Find the page

Objectives

Numeracy
Order whole numbers to at least 100, and position them on a number line.
Use and begin to read the vocabulary of estimation and approximation; give a sensible estimate of at least 50 objects.

Literacy
Use a contents page and index to find their way about a text.

Resources

A class set of a non-fiction book with an index and up to 100 pages; a Big Book with an index for class demonstration.

Vocabulary

number
sequence
estimate
before
after
roughly
first, second, third...

Background
The use of an index to look up references in a book involves both numeracy and literacy skills. We use alphabetical order to locate the required word, and knowledge of numbers to find the referenced page number. The sequence of numbered pages in a book can be compared to a number line. Finding the required page efficiently involves estimating where in the sequence a number is placed: is it near the start, near the end, or near the middle of the book?

Preparation
Distribute the class set of books among the children at the start of the lesson. Prepare a list of topics or entries for the children to look up in the book by using the index. If time allows, compile a list of questions to be answered from the indexed references.

Main teaching activity
Discuss the use of an index with the class, demonstrating the use of alphabetical order to find words of interest. Talk about finding the page numbers that the index provides. *What is the quickest way of doing this? Is it best to flick through the pages from the front, flick through them from the back, or estimate where in the book the page you want is?* Challenge the children to find a specific page number. *Can you estimate where it is before you open the book? How close were you to the right page?* Continue the lesson by asking children to look up the words on

your list and answer questions about them. *Who can find the answer first?*

Differentiation
Follow up the whole-class teaching with paired work in which children with copies of the same book ask each other questions – for example, 'What is the tenth word on page 57?' Less able children should work with books of up to 100 pages.

More able children can search for references in books with many pages, such as encyclopaedias.

Plenary
Conclude the lesson with a discussion of the children's findings. Ask individuals to describe their preferred technique for locating a page. Have they noticed that if they look at the left-hand page numbers while they flick through the book they are all even, but if they look at the right-hand page the numbers are all odd?

Linked to
H i s t o r y

24 Magic squares

Background

'Magic' number squares have been popular with mathematicians through history. Of course, they may not really be 'magic', but nevertheless have intriguing mathematical properties. The key feature of a magic square is that the numbers in all the columns, rows and diagonals add up to the same value. This lesson links the use of magic squares to some historical and geographical work on their origins and beliefs about them. Historical background, and some interactive games suitable for Year 2, can be found on the Internet at *www.mathsyear2000.org/magnet/ kaleidoscope2/MagicSquare/*

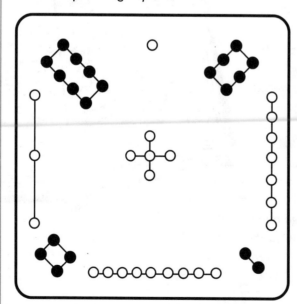

Loh-Shu – the first known 'magic square', believed to have been created more than 5000 years ago in China. The black dots are even numbers, the white dots odd numbers.

(taken from http://www.magic-squares.de/general/squares/ squares.html)

Preparation

Distribute copies of page 161 in advance of the lesson.

Main teaching activity

Introduce the lesson by talking about 'lucky' and 'unlucky' numbers. In many cultures, 7 is regarded as a lucky number whereas 13 is considered unlucky. Explain that there is no mathematical or scientific reason for any number to have 'magical' properties. These beliefs are superstitions, like crossing your fingers or touching wood for luck. Extend the discussion to magic squares. Explain that in ancient China such squares were believed to have magical powers, and were used as good luck charms. Use the first magic square on page 161 to explain the properties of such squares. Ask the children to calculate the sums of the numbers in all the columns and rows, and along the diagonals, to confirm that all of these sums have the same answer. The children should complete the other three magic square exercises on the sheet.

Differentiation

Less able children should concentrate on the first problem: arranging the digits 1, 2 and 3 to form a 3 × 3 magic square.

More able children can extend the exercise to other combinations of digits, including the second and third problems on the sheet. Arranging the digits 1–9 to make a magic square will be a demanding challenge for these children.

Plenary

Ask children to show their completed squares. Check with the class that these are indeed 'magic'. Suggest that the children could reproduce their squares using dots, as in the *Loh-Shu* square shown on the left. Possible solutions for page 161 are:

3	1	2
1	2	3
2	3	1

5	3	4
3	4	5
4	5	3

4	3	8
9	5	1
2	7	6

Solutions in which these arrays of numbers are reflected or rotated also work.

25 Cars on slopes

Objectives

Numeracy
Estimate, measure and compare lengths.
Read a simple scale to the nearest labelled division.
Science
Make and record observations and measurements.
Recognise when a test or comparison is unfair.
Find out about, and describe the movement of, familiar things.
Links to QCA Science Unit 2E: Forces and movement.

Resources

Card or wooden strips, building bricks, a selection of toy cars, tape measures, pencils, paper.

Vocabulary

measure
length
distance
tape measure
centimetre (cm)
record
table

Background

The investigation of the distance travelled by a toy car when it is allowed to roll down a slope onto a smooth surface is a popular science experiment in the primary classroom. Variables that can be controlled include the angle of the slope, the material over which the car runs, and the length of slope down which the car runs. This activity provides an opportunity for developing basic measurement skills, in particular the measurement of length using a tape measure. The children should be encouraged to predict the outcome of their experiment, suggesting how the distance travelled will change in response to changes in the variables they control.

Preparation

Prepare a clear area in the classroom or school hall in which the children can conduct their experiments.

Main teaching activity

Demonstrate how to construct a slope with a card or wooden strip and building bricks. Show how to release a car down the slope.

Encourage the children to observe how the car speeds up as it descends the slope, then gradually slows as it crosses the floor. Ask them to estimate the distance the car travelled before coming to rest. Check their estimates by measuring with the tape measure. Talk about the variables that might affect how far the car travels. Through discussion, establish that the floor surface, the angle of the slope and the length of slope down which the car runs could all affect how far the car runs across the floor. Tell the children that their task is to investigate these factors. At a suitable point in the lesson, introduce the idea of a **fair test** and discuss the importance of changing only one thing at a time.

Set the children to work in groups to make their investigations. They should use a tape measure to record the distance travelled by the car to the nearest centimetre, and record their results in a clear way.

Differentiation

Help less able children to focus on a single variable – for example, changing the height of the slope by supporting the card or wooden strip with one, two or three bricks. Encourage them to record their results in a simple table (an example is shown below).

More able children could extend the investigation to a range of variables. Show them how to present their data in a series of tables, each of which displays how the distance travelled by the car changes with a specific variable.

Number of bricks	Distance travelled by car
1	55cm
2	78cm
3	110cm

Plenary

Review the children's results as a class. Discuss how the groups ensured that their tests were fair.

26 Shape words

Objectives

Numeracy
Use the mathematical names for common 3-D and 2-D shapes. Sort shapes and describe some of their features.

Literacy
Build collections of new words linked to particular topics.

ICT
Explore a variety of ICT tools (for example, word-processing software).

Resources

A computer and word-processing software, a printer. A variety of shape diagrams on separate sheets of paper (see Vocabulary for some examples).

Vocabulary

triangle
circle
square
rectangle
star
pentagon
hexagon
octagon
cube
cuboid
pyramid
sphere
cone
cylinder
point
corner
side
edge

Background

In order to classify and sort shapes, children need to acquire the correct vocabulary. In mathematics, words such as *face*, *edge*, *regular*, *side*, *solid* and *plane* have specific meanings used to describe the features of two-dimensional and three-dimensional shapes. In this activity, the children create a computer word bank of shape names and shape words. The use of this word bank to aid the composition of labels and captions for shape diagrams helps to develop a valuable writing skill.

Preparation

Set up the computer running a word-processing package in advance of the lesson. Photocopy the shape diagrams to distribute copies among the groups.

Main teaching activity

Introduce the lesson by showing the children a selection of shape diagrams. Ask the children to identify the shapes. Discuss their key features. Explain that you are going to 'brainstorm' a list of shape words to create a shape word bank. Act as scribe at the word-processor while the children call out shape names and words. Print copies of the word bank and distribute them for the children to use in their work groups.

In the second part of the lesson, distribute the shape diagrams for the children to annotate. Ask the children to work in pairs or small groups to annotate the shapes they have been given. For each shape, they should write a title, a caption describing the shape and a series of labels with leader lines pointing to its key features. The children can refer to their shape word banks for the correct vocabulary.

Differentiation

Differentiate the activity by varying the complexity of the shape diagrams given to the children. Less able children could annotate diagrams of triangles and squares.

More able children could annotate diagrams of hexagons, octagons and 3-D shapes.

Plenary

Review some of the annotated shape diagrams as a class, reading the titles, captions and labels and checking that these are correct.

Hexagon

side

corner

A hexagon is a 2-D shape. It has six straight sides and six corners.

27 Symmetry

Objectives

Numeracy
Describe the symmetry of 2-D shapes.
Begin to recognise line symmetry.
Science
Explore, using the sense of sight... and make
and record observations.

Resources

A copy of photocopiable page 162 for each
child; a box of safety mirrors; a set of
capital letter cards (these are available
commercially).

Vocabulary

symmetrical
line of symmetry
mirror line
reflection

Background

A shape with **line symmetry** looks unchanged when reflected in a mirror. One half of the shape is the mirror image of the other half. If a mirror is placed along the line that divides the shape into two mirror-image halves, one half of the shape and its reflection appear the same as the complete shape. Such a line is called a **line of symmetry**. A shape such as the letter T has one line of symmetry, a rectangle has two lines of symmetry and a square has four lines of symmetry (see the diagram below). In this activity, the children use a mirror to investigate line symmetry in shapes. Investigating the relationship between a shape and its reflection in a mirror develops skills in scientific observation – for example, the children should observe whether the appearance of a shape is changed by reflection.

Preparation

Distribute copies of page 162 and mirrors on tables in advance of the lesson.

Lines of symmetry

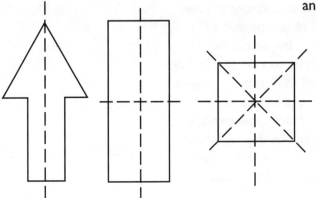

Main teaching activity

Introduce the lesson by talking about reflections. *How do things change when they are reflected? Is your reflection in a mirror exactly the same as you, or is it different in some way?* Use a mirror to demonstrate that left appears to become right on reflection – for example, a watch on the left wrist appears to be on the right wrist when you look in the mirror.

Use a safety mirror and capital letter cards to look at the reflections of letters of the alphabet with the children. *Which letters look the same when reflected? Which letters look back to front?* Explain how we say that shapes that look the same when reflected have **symmetry**. A **line of symmetry** is a line drawn on a shape such that on either side of the line, the halves of the shape are mirror images of each other. Demonstrate how to locate a line of symmetry on a letter by holding a mirror over some letters. For example, A and M have a vertical line of symmetry; B and E have a horizontal line of symmetry; G and Q have no line of symmetry.

Explain that the children are going to investigate the symmetry of different shapes. Set them to work on copies of page 162. They should use safety mirrors to identify which shapes are symmetrical.

Differentiation

Less able children should concentrate on identifying shapes as either symmetrical or not symmetrical. They should tick the symmetrical shapes on page 162.

Challenge more able children to locate and draw the lines of symmetry on the appropriate shapes on page 162.

Plenary

Review the children's findings, discussing the symmetry properties of the shapes on page 162. The heart shape has one line of symmetry; the equilateral triangle has three; the square, cross and star have four; the regular pentagon has five.

Linked to
M u s i c

28 Counting beats

Objectives

Numeracy
Count on in steps of 2, 3, 4, 5 or 10 to at least 30.
Know by heart multiplication facts for the 2 and 10 times tables.
Begin to know multiplication facts for the 5 times table.
Music
To create musical patterns.
Explore, choose and organise sounds and musical ideas.
Links to QCA Music Unit 4.

Resources

A selection of percussion instruments. A copy of photocopiable page 163 for each child.

Vocabulary

count in twos, threes...
pattern
sequence
group

Background

Counting in twos, threes and larger numbers develops children's familiarity with the number patterns required to understand and become proficient at multiplication and division. Counting beats into groups of 2, 3, 4 and 6 (and more rarely 5) establishes different musical rhythms, and is an important skill in musical appreciation and performance. In this lesson, children develop their counting skills together with their awareness of beat and rhythm.

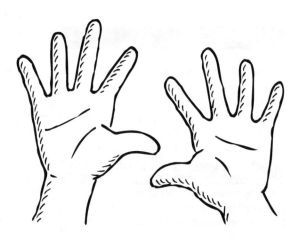

5, with one stress in each group. Explain that in music these divisions are called **bars**. Tap out the 20 beats, emphasising the first beat of the bar in each case, counting 1 2 1 2... 1 2 3 1 2 3... and so on. Ask: *How many bars are there with 2 beats per bar, 4 beats per bar, 5 beats per bar? When there are 3 beats per bar, why do we need 21 beats altogether?*

Differentiation

Let the children spend some time tapping and counting the rhythms for themselves. Suggest that more able children extend the activity to 24 or 30 beats. Ask them to draw dots to represent the beats, and divide them into bars as shown on the photocopiable sheet. *How many 6-beat bars do you need to make 30 beats altogether?*

Plenary

Conclude the lesson with some whole-class rhythmic clapping and counting.

Preparation

Distribute percussion instruments as for a practical music lesson.

Main teaching activity

Start the lesson with some counting practice in various steps. Ask the children to use their fingers to find how many steps must be made to reach a given number (for example 20, 24 or 30) from 0 when they count in twos, threes, fours and so on. For example, ten steps are required to reach 20 when counting in twos, five steps when counting in fours, and four steps when counting in fives.

Give out copies of photocopiable page 163. Ask the children to clap, or tap out, 20 equally spaced beats. Start by counting in ones and tapping out all the beats with equal emphasis, as indicated by the dots that make up the first line on the sheet. Now explain that you are going to tap out the beats with different rhythms. Discuss how the second and subsequent lines on the worksheet divide the 20 beats into groups of 2, 3, 4 and

Linked to
Literacy
ICT

29 Sound puzzles

Background

Creating and solving simple word problems and puzzles involves being able to translate verbal statements into number sentences and vice versa. It thus requires both numeracy and literacy skills. If the problem is recorded on a cassette tape (or a computer hard disk), ICT skills are required as well.

Preparation

Record a sample word puzzle on a cassette tape or computer in advance of the lesson. You might decide to develop a 'birth dates' theme. For example, a puzzle whose answer is a child's date of birth might go as follows:

The day of my birth is twice 8,

The month of my birth is half 20,

The year of my birth is 100 minus 5,

When was I born?

Answer: 16/10/95.

Main teaching activity

Introduce the lesson by talking about the equipment used to record sounds. Show the children the microphone, and explain that it captures the sounds of their voices and converts them into electricity. The electricity travels along the wire that connects the microphone to the tape recorder or computer, and the sound is recorded on the cassette tape or computer disk. It can then be played back through the loudspeaker as

many times as you like. Ask: *Do any of you have counting, times tables or puzzle tapes at home? Do they help you with your maths?*

Play the sample puzzle to the whole class and help them to solve it. Explain that the children should each write their own puzzle, using addition, subtraction, multiplication and division as they wish. Set the children to compose their puzzles with pencil and paper. When they have done so, ask them to record their puzzles on the cassette tape or computer. If a computer is used, save each sound file with its author's name. Organise all the sound puzzles in a puzzle folder. The children will enjoy opening and listening to their own and others' sound files in subsequent numeracy or ICT lessons.

Differentiation

Less able children could write simple puzzles based on their age in years.

More able children could devise puzzles involving more complex calculations.

Plenary

Play some of the recorded puzzles to the whole class and solve them together.

Linked to
D & T

30 Count the bricks

Objectives

Numeracy
Know what each digit in a two-digit number represents, including zero as a place holder, and partition two-digit numbers into a multiple of ten and ones (TU).
Use and begin to read the vocabulary of comparing and ordering numbers, including ordinal numbers to 100.
Compare two given two-digit numbers, say which is more or less, and give a number that lies between them.

Design and technology
Select materials for making their product.
Carry out design and make assignments using… items that can be put together to make products.
Links to QCA Design and technology Units 1B and 1D.

Resources

Boxes of mixed construction bricks, containing no more than 100 bricks of any one colour or type; a story or short non-fiction book about building a house (such as *Bricks* by Terry Cash, A&C Black).

Vocabulary

units
ones
tens
digit
two-digit number
teens number
more
fewer
less
order
between

Background

To use the decimal number system correctly, we need to understand the importance of place value and the use of 0 as a place holder. These two features of the number system become significant as soon as children start to write two-digit numbers using tens and units. Children need to understand that in a number such as 33, the first 3 stands for three lots of ten while the second 3 stands for three units. In this lesson, the children sort construction bricks by colour and count them by grouping them in tens and units. They compare numbers of different-coloured bricks, say which of two numbers is more or less, and are prompted to suggest a number that lies between. This work is linked to the planning stage of work with a construction kit in a design and technology project.

Preparation

Set out boxes of construction bricks.

Main teaching activity

Introduce the lesson by reading a story or short non-fiction book about building a house (see Resources) to the whole class. Explain that their task during this lesson is to sort and count the construction bricks in preparation for their own model house-building activities. Demonstrate how to sort the bricks by colour and count them by making groups of 10, then counting the number of groups of ten plus any units that total less than 10. The number of bricks is given by these two digits: the number of tens and the number of units. Set each group to sort and count the bricks in one box.

Differentiation

Make sure that less able children are grouping the bricks correctly in tens.

Ask more able children to organise the sets of counted bricks in sequence of number and make a table to show the number of each colour available in their box.

Plenary

Reinforce the concept of tens and units through discussion of some of the sets of bricks that the children have set out on the tables. Compare different sets using vocabulary such as *more, less, fewer* and *in between*.

31 Sound sums

Objectives

Numeracy
Use known number facts and place value to add/subtract mentally.
Use known number facts and place value to carry out mentally simple multiplications and divisions.
Literacy
Write non-fiction texts.
ICT
Enter and store information in a variety of forms.

Resources

Cassette recorders with microphones (or a computer with sound recording software and a microphone); pencils, paper.

Vocabulary

puzzle
solve
calculate
answer
right
wrong
How did you work it out?
number sentence

Background

This activity builds on Lesson 29, 'Sound puzzles'. The children use the same approach as before to record and solve mental maths addition, subtraction, multiplication and division problems. This activity could be used at several points during the year to develop and reinforce the various mental maths skills outlined in the National Numeracy Strategy objectives and examples. Making sound recordings on cassette tapes or computers develops the children's ICT skills. To link with work in literacy, encourage the children to formulate their questions as story problems.

Preparation

Record some sample problems onto a cassette tape or computer in advance of the lesson. You could record a series of straightforward calculations, such as *Thirty plus six* and *Seventy-six minus forty*, or produce story problems such as *There are 24 books. Shane takes nine and Sophie takes three. How many are left?* Leave plenty of time between the problems to let the children formulate answers. Alternatively, use a bell or bleeper at the end of each problem to indicate that the playback should be paused until the children have written down or given their answer.

Main teaching activity

Play the sample problems to the whole class

and solve them together. Explain that the children are going to set and record their own addition, subtraction, multiplication or division problems. Set them to compose a series of problems based on mental maths strategies that you are currently developing as a class. They should write out their problems using pencil and paper.

As the children complete their problems, check and discuss them. Now ask the children to record selected problems on the cassette tape or computer. If a computer is used, save each sound file with its author's name. Encourage children with good computer skills to do this for themselves. Organise all the sound puzzles in a puzzle folder. The children will enjoy opening and listening to their own and others' sound files in subsequent numeracy or ICT lessons.

Differentiation

Children should write problems appropriate to their level of mathematical skill. More able children could be given the responsibility of organising the recordings or sound files for others to use.

Plenary

Play some of the recorded problems to the whole class and solve them together.

Linked to
Literacy
Geography

32 School trip

Objectives

Numeracy
Choose and use appropriate operations and efficient calculation strategies to solve problems.
Solve simple word problems involving numbers in 'real life'.
English
Write notes and messages.
Geography
Recognise how places compare with other places.
Links to QCA Geography Unit 4.

Resources

A copy of photocopiable page 164 for each child; a map of the local area, showing possible venues for a school trip.

Vocabulary

time
how long
hour
cost
money
distance
far

Background

Mathematics plays an important role in planning and organising a real-life travel experience such as a school trip. In this lesson, the children use the mathematics of number, distance, money and time to plan a school trip. They also complete a note to their parents explaining how the trip will be organised. The activity links work in mathematics to the use of geography and literacy skills.

Preparation

Set up or draw a local map and identify some possible venues for a school trip. Compile a list of distances and travel times to the different locations on the board. Distribute copies of page 164.

Main teaching activity

Introduce the lesson by explaining that the children are going to choose a venue for a possible class trip, plan the outing and complete a letter to their parents explaining details of the trip.

Look at the map and discuss possible venues. Debate the merits of the various locations and talk through the necessary planning. Prompt discussion of distance, travel time, activities, pocket money, adult helpers, size of bus needed and costs.

Photocopiable page 164 provides an outline letter describing the school trip to parents. Explain that the children should choose their preferred destination from the options you have discussed, then fill in the details in the blank spaces on the letter.

Differentiation

Less able children should concentrate on filling in the basic details on the sheet.

Encourage more able children to extend their planning. They could research information such as opening times, local bus companies and entry costs, perhaps with the aid of the Internet.

Plenary

Review some of the children's completed letters as a class. Discuss the relative costs and other advantages or disadvantages of the alternative trips.

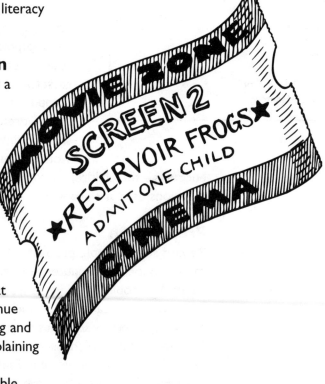

Linked to
Geography

33 Lucky numbers

Background

As children count from zero in twos, fives and tens, the patterns in the number sequences will become familiar. Counting in twos from zero produces the sequence of even numbers; counting in fives produces a sequence of numbers that end alternately in 0 and 5; counting in tens produces a sequence of numbers that end in 0. These number sequences are the multiples of 2, 5 and 10 respectively. Picking a 'lucky number' to win a prize is a common feature of seaside piers, fêtes and fairgrounds; the activity can be set in this context, linking to geography or history work on holidays. The children make a 'lucky number' draw in which the prize-winning numbers are multiples of, for example, 5 or 10.

Preparation

Set out the resources on tables in advance of the lesson.

Main teaching activity

Begin the lesson with some whole-class counting practice in twos, fives, tens and other intervals. Point to the numbers on the square as you count together. Explain that the numbers in the sequence 2, 4, 6, 8... are called **even numbers**. Can the children spot the patterns in the number sequences produced by counting in fives and tens? Explain that these numbers are called **multiples** of 5 and 10 respectively.

Ask the children about number games at fairs and fêtes they have visited. What are the good and bad points of these places or events? Talk about raffles, tombolas, Bingo and other number games. What happens to the money paid to enter these games? Is it all returned as prizes? If not – where does it go? Is the extra money raised for charity – or is it profit for the stall-holder?

Ask the children to make a lucky number game. They can devise their own rules. Suggest that the 'lucky numbers' could be those ending in 5 or 0. The children should devise their games in groups, either making their own numbered tickets or using tickets you have provided.

Differentiation

Less able children could make a game with tickets numbered 0–20, perhaps deciding that even-numbered tickets are prize winners.

More able children could extend their ticket numbers to 100 and beyond, and establish their own rules for winners. Make sure they discuss the proportion of winning tickets that their chosen rules will produce. For example, if they decide that tickets ending in zero are 'lucky', then one ticket in ten will be a winner.

Plenary

Play the children's 'lucky number' games with the whole class. Ask representatives to explain their rules and to decide, with the help of the number square, how many prizes they will need if they sell all the tickets. Talk about running the game at a school fair. *How much should the ticket price be?* Explain that if the prizes are donated (for example, by parents), the money collected can all go to the school fund or a chosen charity.

34 Fruit fractions

Objectives

Numeracy
Begin to recognise and find one half and one quarter of shapes and small numbers of objects.
Begin to recognise that two halves or four quarters make one whole, and that two quarters and one half are equivalent.
Design and technology
Measure, mark out, cut and shape a range of materials.
Builds on QCA D&T Unit 1C: Eat more fruit and vegetables.

Resources

A disc of modelling clay on a tray to represent a pizza; eight clay 'olives'; a copy of photocopiable page 165 for each child; adhesive, paper, scissors; washed grapes and strawberries, plastic dishes, a chopping board, dessert knives (not sharp); kitchen facilities; an adult helper.

Vocabulary

part
equal parts
fraction
one whole
one half
two halves
one quarter, two... three... four quarters

Background

The idea of fractions can be introduced through the process of dividing a whole into parts in order to share – for example, dividing an apple in half to share between two children, or dividing a pizza into halves and then quarters to share fairly between a family of four. This process is best introduced with plenty of visual or practical examples. Divide squares and other shapes into halves on the board, then divide them into halves again to produce quarters. Cutting fruit in a design and technology activity is an excellent opportunity to demonstrate halving and quartering.

Preparation

Set the scissors and copies of page 165 on tables. Prepare the fruit and kitchen items in the kitchen area for small groups, working with an adult helper.

Main teaching activity

Introduce the lesson by discussing and demonstrating the division of the clay 'pizza' into halves and quarters. Count the halves and quarters. Demonstrate that two quarters equal one half and that the halves are identical, as are the quarters. Share the eight 'olives' between the pizza portions, explaining how each slice has one quarter (two) of the olives.

Set the children to work in groups on the photocopiable sheet. They should cut out the

shapes and divide them into fractions as indicated, then arrange the parts and stick them onto backing paper for display. The children should label the halves and quarters appropriately. While the majority of the groups are completing this activity, groups can take turns to prepare fruit salad with the adult helper. Normal hygiene and safety procedures for working with food in a kitchen area must be followed. The children could cut grapes in half and strawberries in quarters to make their fruit salads.

Differentiation

Make sure that less able children understand that two halves must be equal, and that four quarters must also be equal. Ask them to make sure that they have divided the fruit 'fairly'.

Introduce more able children to the ideas and vocabulary of quarters: *two quarters make a half; three-quarters; four quarters make a whole.* If they are ready, discuss the division of a whole into other fractions, such as thirds and fifths.

Plenary

Review the children's work by making a display of their completed fraction activity sheets. Share some of the fruit salad. Discuss whether each piece you eat is the whole fruit, half of the fruit or a quarter of the fruit!

Linked to
H i s t o r y
G e o g r a p h y

 # Clocks and watches

Objectives

Numeracy
Read the time to the hour, half-hour or quarter-hour on an analogue clock and a 12-hour digital clock, and understand the notation 7:30.
History
Use common words and phrases relating to the passing of time.
Geography
Make observations about where things are located.
Builds on QCA Geography Unit 1.

Resources

Demonstration analogue and digital clock faces; a clock that chimes the hour, half hour and quarter hours, or a recording of such a clock (alternatively, a recording of the chimes of Big Ben); a copy of photocopiable page 166 for each child.

Vocabulary

clock
analogue
digital
o'clock
half past
quarter past
quarter to

Background

In Year 2 (Primary 3), children should begin to read analogue clocks and 12-hour digital clocks to the nearest quarter-hour. In this activity, children are introduced to digital clock displays and compare them with analogue clock displays. Clock faces are often significant landmarks, appearing on historic buildings such as Big Ben. Before the days of cheap clocks and watches, many people kept track of time by listening to the chimes of a local church clock. Examples of both analogue and digital clock faces can be seen in most towns and cities. A survey of clocks on churches and other buildings could be undertaken as part of children's work on the geography and history of their local environment.

Preparation

Set up the clock faces where they can be seen by the whole class. Distribute copies of page 166 in advance of the lesson.

Main teaching activity

Introduce the lesson with a chiming clock or a recording of such a clock. Demonstrate how the clock chimes the hour, half-hour and quarter-hours. Discuss the children's experience of the Houses of Parliament on visits or on television. Do they know of any chiming clocks in their locality? Use an analogue clock face to work through the vocabulary of hours, half-hours and quarter-hours: *10 o'clock, quarter past 10, half past 10, quarter to 11...* Introduce the alternative vocabulary that has developed from the use of digital clocks, demonstrating the relevant times on a digital clock face: *10 o'clock, ten-fifteen, ten-thirty, ten forty-five...* Set the children to complete the activity on the photocopiable sheet, filling in the times using the notation you have introduced.

Differentiation

Make sure that all the children can read the time to the nearest hour and half-hour. Ask less able children to set the hands of the demonstration clock on the hour, at half past the hour and finally at quarter past and quarter to the hour.

More able children should begin to read the time to the nearest minute.

Plenary

Review the answers to page 166: half past four, half past one, half past nine, half past twelve, half past five, half past three, eight o'clock, four-thirty, ten-thirty, eleven o'clock, three-thirty, six-thirty, five o'clock, twelve-thirty.

Discuss any clocks that the children might have seen in the local environment. Are there any chiming church clocks nearby?

36 Assessment 2

Objectives

The assessment activities in this book are designed to introduce Key Stage 1 children to SAT-style questions. They are set in cross-curricular contexts based on the preceding term's lessons. The questions in Assessment 2 test the children's progress in: sequencing numbers to 100; solving number puzzles; and recognising mathematical shapes.

Resources

One copy per child of photocopiable page 167, pencils; twenty pencils or similar objects for counting.

Preparation

Make copies of the assessment sheet in advance of the lesson. If you feel that the sheet is too 'busy', the three activities could be separated and enlarged on individual sheets.

Lesson introduction

Begin the assessment lesson by reviewing the relevant cross-curricular topics covered during the term. Remind the children of some of the projects and investigations they have undertaken, and ask them to recall and recount their work. Emphasise the mathematical content – for example, *Do you remember how the numbers were arranged in sequence on the Bingo cards?*

Main assessment activity

Distribute the sheets and ask the children to work on them individually. Guide the whole class through the questions one at a time, reading the text with them, and prompting them to work out and fill in their answers. Try to make the whole activity enjoyable!

Practical activity

Set out a group of nine pencils and a second group of five. Tell the child a number story based on the sets: *Salma has nine pencils, Joe has five pencils. Altogether, Salma and Joe have 14 pencils.* Set out two new groups of pencils and ask the child to tell you a number story of the same type.

Set out a group of 12 pencils and tell a subtraction number story: *Joe has 12 pencils. He gives five to Salma. Joe has seven pencils left.* Ask the child to make up a similar number story.

Plenary

Review the answers to the questions as a class. Collect the completed question sheets to use as an aid to judging individual children's progress, and to include in your records. The answers are:

2	7	6
9	5	1
4	3	8

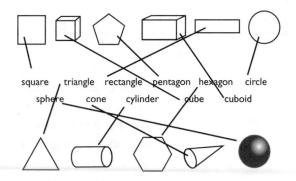

square   triangle   rectangle   pentagon   hexagon   circle
sphere   cone   cylinder   cube   cuboid

	12	21	33	42		60	72	82	
2	13		34		56	66	74	85	91
5	17	24		45	58		77		96
8		29	37	48	59	68		89	99

37 Numbers and words

Objectives

Numeracy
Read and write whole numbers to at least 100 in figures and words.
Literacy
Read on sight and spell high-frequency words.

Resources

A copy of photocopiable page 168 for each child; a chart listing the numbers 0–100 in numerals and in words; a board or flip chart.

Vocabulary

zero, one, two, three... twenty (and beyond)

Background

Reading numerals as words can be quite a challenge, since there are no phonic clues to follow. We cannot expect a child to know that 5, 15 and 50 must be read as 'five', 'fifteen' and 'fifty' without having first heard the words spoken at the same time as seeing the numerals and number words. In this lesson, children make the link between the spoken and written forms of the numbers to 100, then practise translating from one form to another. Reading numerals and number words on sight is also an important literacy skill.

Preparation

Display the number chart where it can be seen easily by all the children. Distribute copies of page 168.

Main teaching activity

Introduce the lesson by talking about numbers in everyday life. Where do the children hear numbers to 100 (and beyond) spoken, or see them written? They may suggest house numbers, raffle ticket numbers, snooker and darts scores, cricket scores, locker numbers and so on.

Continue the lesson with some whole-class counting practice. Count in ones, twos, fives, tens and other intervals, pointing to the numerals and words on the chart as the children count aloud. Explain that you are going to practise writing numbers in two different ways: as **numerals** and as words. Write some examples of numbers to 100 as numerals and as words on the board or flip chart. Review some of the patterns

that appear when numbers are written in words, for example the 'teen' numbers and the multiples of ten. Use the number names *twenty-two*, *thirty-three*, *forty-four* and *fifty-five* to reinforce the difference in spelling between some 'unit' numbers and the corresponding 'tens' numbers. Ask the children to complete the photocopiable sheet, working individually.

Differentiation

Make sure that less able children can write the numbers up to 20 as numerals and words correctly before they progress to the numbers (beyond 20) on the activity sheet.

More able children can be challenged to write numbers greater than 100 in words.

Plenary

Review the answers to page 168 with the whole class. Write selected answers on the board or flip chart.

Linked to
L i t e r a c y

38 Months and seasons

Objectives

Numeracy
Order the months of the year
Literacy
Read on sight high-frequency words, including the months of the year.

Resources

Copies of photocopiable pages 12 and 169 for each group, scissors; a wall display of the months of the year; ordinal number cards up to '12th' (from resource page 13).

Vocabulary

first, second, third...
January, February, March...
spring, summer, autumn, winter

Background

In Year 2 (Primary 3), children should learn the names and order of the months of the year. This lesson builds on Lesson 4, which used the sequence of days in the week to introduce ordinal numbers. The months of the year are included in the list of high-frequency 'read on sight' words in the National Literacy Strategy *Framework for Teaching*. Links can be made to several other curriculum areas, including science and geography (weather and the seasons), history (origins of the names of the months) and RE (festivals and celebrations).

Preparation

Distribute copies of page 169 and scissors on the tables.

Main teaching activity

Read the names of the months of the year on the wall display as a whole class. Use the ordinal number cards to match the months to their ordinal numbers. Ask the children to name the current month and tell you its number.

Ask a series of questions such as:
● *Which is the seventh month of the year?*
● *The second month of the year is February.*
● *What number month is June?*

Talk about the seasons and the weather that we usually expect to have in the different months. Set the children to work in groups with the photocopiable sheets. They need to cut out the month and season names from page 12, turn them over and shuffle them, then take turns to pick up a month or season and place it in the correct box on page 169.

Differentiation

Less able children should concentrate on sequencing the month names in the correct order.

More able children can play a game in which they take turns to select a month name card at random and try to recall the month's number as quickly as possible.

Plenary

Use the plenary session to develop cross-curricular links. For example, you could discuss the characteristics of the seasons in more detail (science), or discuss the origin of the names of the months (history). These ideas could be developed in a follow-up literacy lesson, for example by writing class poems based on the sequences of the seasons and months (these could be arranged as circular wall displays).

39 Measure it!

Objectives

Numeracy
Use the vocabulary related to length and time.
Measure and compare lengths.
Use units of time.

PE
Explore basic skills, actions and ideas with increasing understanding.
Describe what they have done.
Travel with, send and receive a ball and other equipment in different ways.

Resources

Beanbags, tape measures, digital stopwatches, notepads, pencils.

Vocabulary

estimate
measure
compare
far, further, furthest
metre (m), centimetre (cm)
tape measure
second, minute

Background

Measuring distances and times is significant for many sports activities, especially track and field athletics. PE lessons provide numerous opportunities for developing and applying measurement skills – for example, measurement of times taken and distances thrown or jumped.

Preparation

Prepare for an outdoor PE lesson according to your normal practice.

Main teaching activity

Introduce the PE lesson with a discussion of the children's jumping and throwing skills. *How far can you throw a beanbag? Can you throw it one centimetre? One metre? Ten metres? A hundred metres?* Develop a discussion by considering how far the children think they can jump.

Divide the class into pairs and give each child a beanbag. Ask the children to take turns to predict how far they will be able to throw the beanbag. One child should stand still and the second child place a bean bag to mark the predicted distance. The first child should then throw his or her beanbag. The children should measure and record the two distances: the prediction and the actual result. They should swap roles and repeat. Ask each pair: *How accurate were your predictions? Were they too high or too low?*

Each pair should now repeat the whole activity, but this time predict and check the distances they can jump. They could extend this to other predictions and measurements, such as the distance run in five seconds or the time taken to sit down and stand up ten times.

Differentiation

Less able children should concentrate on making direct comparisons (without measuring) between their predictions and their actual achievements.

Encourage more able children to predict, then measure and record their performances with a tape measure and a stopwatch.

Plenary

Discuss the children's findings as a class. *How far can most of you throw or jump? How long would it take most of you to run 100 metres? Could any human being jump 50 metres or run 100 metres in five seconds?*

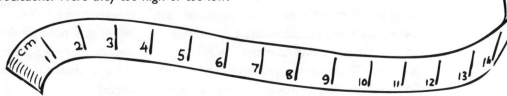

Linked to
D & T

40 Wind it up!

Objectives

Numeracy
Estimate, measure and compare lengths.
Recognise whole, half and quarter turns, to
the left or right, clockwise or anticlockwise.
Design and technology
Be taught how mechanisms can be
used in different ways.
Carry out focused practical tasks.
**Links to QCA Design and technology Unit
2C: Winding up.**

Resources

A copy of photocopiable page 170 for each
child; Pringles potato crisp tubes, thick card,
adhesive tape, glue, lengths of dowel, string,
pencils, plastic spiders; rulers; a board or
flip chart.

Vocabulary

turn
quarter turn
half turn
clockwise
anticlockwise

Background

Clocks, pencil
sharpeners, bicycles
and many other
simple machines and
vehicles have parts
that turn. The
mathematics of
rotation and turning
includes concepts
such as a whole turn,
a half turn, a quarter
turn (a right angle)
and the direction of
turn – clockwise or
anticlockwise. In this
activity, the children
follow instructions to
make a
simple
wind-
up
spider
toy. The
toy can
be used
to investigate turning motion and the
connection between the number of turns
and the distance the spider rises.

Preparation

Prepare a set of materials for each group to
make a 'spider winder' in advance of the
lesson. The materials needed are listed in the
'You will need' section on page 170. All
cutting that requires sharp scissors or knives
must be done by an adult in advance of the
lesson. Prepare the classroom for a practical
technology lesson according to your normal
practice. Provide a copy of page 170 on each
table with a set of construction materials.

Main teaching activity

Start the lesson by talking about mechanical
things that turn – for example, clocks, wheels,
pulleys, drills and roundabouts. Explain that
the children are going to make a wind-up
spider toy. Show them the activity sheet and
the materials. Read through the instructions

together before
starting. Set the
children to make
their toys, providing
help with gluing
and assembly as
necessary.

Differentiation

Some children will need a considerable
amount of help to produce a working toy.
Encourage more able children to
decorate their toys, and to consider possible
improvements or alternative designs (for
example, mounting the winder on a handle
like a fishing rod, so that it can be held more
easily).

Plenary

Use the toys as the basis for some
mathematical investigations. *Which way must
you turn the handle to wind the spider up?
Which way to let the spider fall down? If the
handle starts at the top, where is it after a
quarter turn/a half turn?* Use a ruler to
investigate how far the spider rises with one,
two or more whole turns. *How would this
distance change if the winder were smaller/
larger?*

41 Make a scale

Objectives

Numeracy
Order whole numbers to at least 100, and position them on a number line.
Use and begin to read the vocabulary of estimation and approximation; give a sensible estimate of at least 50 objects.
Read a simple scale to the nearest labelled division.

Science
Collect evidence by making observations and measurements.
Make simple comparisons and identify simple patterns or associations.

Resources

A tray for each group, containing 100 identical plastic cubes, small building bricks or beads; tall clear plastic containers with parallel sides (these could be made by cutting the tops off plastic lemonade bottles); rulers, felt-tip pens.

Vocabulary

estimate
roughly
close to
exactly
measure
compare
container
contain

Background

Measuring scales, such as those on rulers and containers, are good examples of number lines. The process of reading a scale is a practical application of finding the position of a number on a number line. In order to create a measuring scale, children need to order and position numbers along a line. There is a clear link between the mathematical skills involved in using a number line and the use of measuring scales in science activities. This lesson also develops the children's ability to estimate a number of objects.

Preparation

Set out plastic containers, trays of bricks (or similar items), pens and rulers on the tables in preparation for group work.

Main teaching activity

Explain that the children's task is to make a 'brick measuring cylinder'. Show the class an empty plastic container, then fill the container with bricks from a tray. State that it now holds 100 bricks. Ask the children to tell you how the container might be used in future to measure out sets of approximately 100 bricks at a time. Lead them to suggest that you should make a mark showing the level of the bricks in the container, and label it '100'. Now ask them to suggest how you could make marks to measure out smaller quantities of bricks – for example, you should fill the container halfway up to the

100 mark for 50 bricks. The children should eventually arrive at the idea of a measuring scale that is marked and labelled up the side of the container.

Set the children to work in groups to produce their own brick measuring devices. They should add 10 bricks at a time to the container, marking and labelling the level at each stage.

Differentiation

Challenge more able children by asking them to produce different measuring cylinders for a variety of different-sized objects, extending their scales beyond 100 where appropriate.

Plenary

Use the plenary session to check (by counting measured samples of bricks) and discuss the accuracy of the scales that the children have produced. Explain that they should not expect their scales to be perfectly accurate, but only to give a good 'estimate' of the number of bricks in a sample, because the bricks pile up slightly differently each time you fill the container.

Linked to
D & T

42 Climbing frames

Objectives

Numeracy
Use the mathematical names for common 3-D and 2-D shapes.
Make and describe shapes.
Design and technology
Develop ideas by putting together components.
Communicate their ideas using a variety of methods, including making models.
Links to QCA Design and technology Unit 1B: Playgrounds.

Resources

Rod and joint construction kits (such as K'nex); alternatively, frameworks can be constructed by joining plastic straws with pipe-cleaners or adhesive tape.

Vocabulary

shape
frame
edge
side
make
build
corner
cube
cuboid
pyramid
triangle
square
rectangle
pentagon
hexagon
octagon

Background

Climbing frames are constructed by joining rods, tubes or bars into three-dimensional frameworks. The shapes created range from simple triangular 'A' frames used to support swings, through cuboids and pyramids, to complex domes of linked hexagons and pentagons (similar to the pattern of shapes used to make a football from leather patches). In this activity, the children identify and describe the shapes they find in climbing frames and other apparatus around the school, then design their own model climbing frames using construction toys. The lesson links work on the mathematics of shapes to their use in a design and technology project.

Preparation

Set out the construction materials on the tables in advance of the lesson.

Main teaching activity

Introduce the lesson by taking the children outside to examine climbing frames and other apparatus in the school grounds. Talk about the construction and shape of the frameworks, using the names of 3-D shapes such as 'cuboid' and 'pyramid', and identify the basic 2-D shapes (such as triangles and rectangles) from which they are composed.

Return to the classroom and explain that the children are going to design their own climbing frames using the construction materials provided. Discuss how to make basic 2-D shapes, including triangles and squares, from the kit components, and demonstrate how these can be linked together to form a 3-D framework. Set the children to work in small groups on the construction project.

Differentiation

The children will be differentiated by the complexity of both their designs and the language they use to describe the shapes that their designs contain.

Plenary

Ask representatives from the groups to show and describe the climbing frames they have produced. Prompt them to use the vocabulary of shape to describe the key features of their structures.

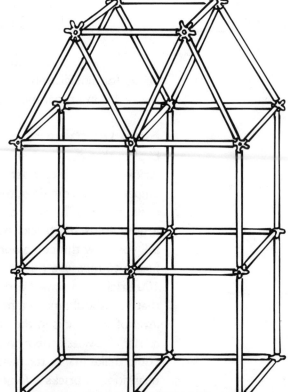

Linked to
History

43 The lady with the lamp

Objectives

Numeracy
Order whole numbers to at least 100, and position them on a number line.
Use the vocabulary related to time.
History
Study the lives of significant men, women and children drawn from the history of Britain and the wider world.
Place events in chronological order.
Links to QCA History Unit 4.

Resources

A copy of photocopiable page 171 for each child, scissors, glue, pencils.

Vocabulary

number line
order
sequence
year
century

Background

Constructing a timeline helps children to appreciate the sequence of historical events, both in the lives of individuals and more generally in the history of Britain and the wider world. It is also an exercise in sequencing numbers on a number line. Children in Year 2 (Primary 3) are only required to sequence numbers to 100; but in the context of history, year numbers such as 1820 and 1910 should be accessible to the children. In this activity, some events in the life of Florence Nightingale are sequenced on a number line showing both her age (the numbers 0–90) and the calendar year (the numbers 1820–1910). Identifying the relationship between these two time scales should help the children to understand the link between the changing date and the passage of time.

Preparation

This lesson should build on a previous history lesson in which the life and work of Florence Nightingale have been introduced. Distribute copies of page 171.

Main teaching activity

The boxes on the photocopiable sheet record some significant events in the life of Florence Nightingale, giving her age when they took place. Discuss the events in her life with the class. Set the children the task of cutting out the event boxes and arranging them in the correct sequence along the timeline. They should draw an arrow to link each event to the timeline, showing as

accurately as possible the year in which the event took place.

Differentiation

Less able children should concentrate on sequencing the seven events correctly.

You could ask more able children who have completed the activity rapidly to research and construct a similar timeline for a famous person of their choice.

Plenary

Review the answers to page 171 with the whole class. The correct dates for the events are: felt called by God to do special work, 1837; decided to nurse the sick, 1845; went to the Crimea to nurse soldiers, 1854; returned to England, 1856; founded school for nurses, 1860; died, 1910. What do the children think they might be doing at the ages given in the seven event boxes?

44 Count the stairs

Objectives

Numeracy
Say the number names in order to at least 100.
Describe and extend simple number sequences: count on in twos.
History
Study past events from the history of Britain and the wider world.
Links to QCA History Unit 5.

Resources

A strip of stiff card (3cm × 40cm) for each child; pencils, rulers, felt-tip pens; a picture showing a cross-section of the stairs in St Paul's Cathedral, London.

Vocabulary

count
sequence
count in ones
count in twos
how many?
zero

Background

On visits to historic buildings such as St Paul's Cathedral, children love to climb and count the stairs. Cross-sections of the cathedral showing the numbers of steps to the various galleries are readily available, and could be displayed in the classroom as part of work on Sir Christopher Wren and the rebuilding of London after the Great Fire. Some towns have long flights of stone steps on hillsides. Making a model of the staircase in St Paul's Cathedral places the use of counting skills in the context of an historical investigation. When the opportunity arises, count stairs with children as you climb them – either in ones (at each step) or in twos (at every other step).

Preparation

Set out the card strips and other resources on tables ready for the children's practical work. Clear a large display area on one of the classroom walls and prepare it with backing paper.

Main teaching activity

Talk about long flights of stairs that the children have climbed. Describe the climb to the Whispering Gallery and beyond in St Paul's Cathedral, which would make an exciting expedition for a child. Some children may have made this ascent with their parents on visits to London. Show the children a cross-section picture of the staircase, and read off the numbers of stairs to different points in the dome.

Explain that the children are going to make a model of the stairway – but there are so many stairs that they will have to make just 20 each. Show them how to rule their card strips and number them as shown in the illustration below. Assign each child a starting number in order to produce a continuous number line. When the children have ruled and numbered their strips, show them how to fold the strip to make a section of the stairway. Ask each child to count his or her stairs in ones and twos from the starting number.

Differentiation

Assign less able children sequences of numbers below 100 to label their stairs with.
More able children can be assigned sequences of higher numbers.

Plenary

As a class, assemble the complete stairway along one wall of the classroom, fixing each section in place with adhesive tape on backing paper. Label every tenth step, and indicate the locations of different features in St Paul's Cathedral next to the stairway. Encourage the children to use this stairway for counting whenever the opportunity arises.

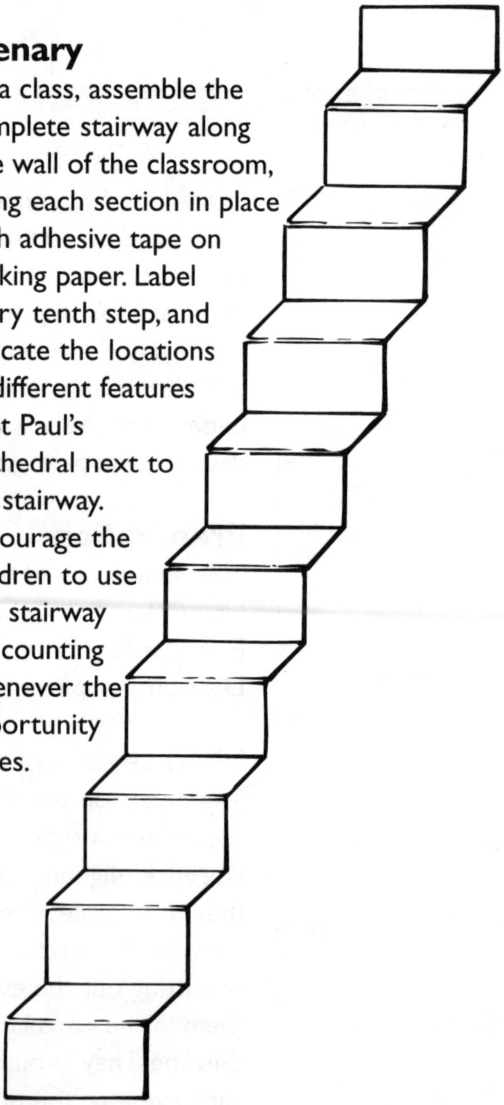

Linked to
Science

45 Making biscuits

Objectives

Numeracy
Know by heart doubles of all numbers to 10 and the corresponding halves.
Solve mathematical problems, recognise simple patterns and relationships.
Use simple multiplication and division to solve... problems involving numbers in 'real life' or measures.

Science
Make and record observations and measurements.
Explore and describe the way some everyday materials change when they are heated.

Resources

Ingredients, measuring cups and spoons to make up the biscuit recipe shown opposite; a board or flip chart; adult help and a school teaching kitchen for follow-up science and technology lessons.

Vocabulary

measure
double
halve
quantity
amount

Background

Cooking provides opportunities for linking work in several areas of the curriculum. The ingredients must be measured (mathematics); they must be mixed and moulded to shape (technology); as the ingredients are mixed and baked, changes in their properties can be observed (science). In this lesson, children look closely at a biscuit recipe and discuss how it could be modified to bake different quantities. With appropriate adult help, the children could make their own biscuits in follow-up science and technology lessons.

Preparation

Prepare the ingredients and set them out for demonstration to the class. Write the recipe and instructions on the board for the whole class to see. Follow normal classroom safety and hygiene procedures for cooking activities.

Main teaching activity

Show the class the recipe and the ingredients. Discuss the changes in the materials that happen as the ingredients are mixed and the biscuits are cooked. Ask:
Which part of the process makes the greatest difference to the ingredients?

Explain that the recipe makes 20 biscuits. Ask the children what changes would be needed to make 10, 40, 60 or more biscuits. Encourage them to use the vocabulary of doubling and halving to adjust the quantities.

GINGER BISCUITS

To make 20 biscuits, you need:

3 cups plain flour
1 cup sugar
2 tbsp soft margarine
1 tsp baking powder
1 tsp ground ginger
4 tbsp cold water
a greased baking tray
an oven
a spoon
a chopping board
a bowl

INSTRUCTIONS
1. Wash and dry your hands.

2. Mix the flour, sugar, ginger and baking powder in the bowl.

3. Rub the margarine into the other ingredients with your fingers.

4. Add a little water and press the mixture into a ball. Put the ball onto a board and cut into 20 pieces. Roll each piece into a small ball and press it flat on the baking tray.

5. Bake the biscuits in a hot oven (180°C) for about 20 minutes.

Complete the lesson by measuring and mixing the ingredients for 20 biscuits in front of the children. They should count the spoons and cups as they are measured, then count the biscuits as they are rolled out and placed on the baking tray.

Differentiation

Challenge more able children with questions about doubling or halving the quantities.

Less able children should count the basic measures and the number of biscuits produced.

Plenary

Cook, count and finally eat the biscuits!

Linked to
ICT
Literacy

46 Maze masters

Numeracy
Give instructions for moving along a route in straight lines and around right-angled corners: for example, to pass through a simple maze.
English
Listen to retellings of traditional stories.
ICT
Plan and give instructions to make things happen.
Explore a variety of ICT tools.
Links to QCA ICT Unit 2D Routes: controlling a floor turtle.

Resources

A copy of photocopiable page 172 for each child.

Vocabulary

forwards
backwards
turn
right, left
clockwise, anticlockwise
right angle
half turn
quarter turn
degrees

Background
Programmable floor robots and computer turtle graphics introduce children to the process of issuing a series of commands in order to produce a desired result. The movements of a robot or turtle develop children's understanding of the relative sizes of numbers (in the context of measures) and the vocabulary of turning. In this activity, the children issue a series of instructions to help a partner find the way through a maze. The lesson is set in the context of the Ancient Greek story of Theseus and the Minotaur.

Preparation
Distribute copies of page 172 in advance of the lesson.

Main teaching activity
Introduce the lesson by telling the story of Theseus and the Minotaur. Discuss mazes the children may have visited – for example, the one at Hampton Court Palace. Explain that at a public maze, there is often a high platform from which the 'maze keeper' can give instructions to people who are lost in order to help them get out of the maze.

Explain that the children's task is to give instructions so that their friend, who is stuck in a maze, can escape. But they should take care not to lead their friend to a Minotaur by accident! Look at the maze on the activity sheet and discuss how to issue appropriate instructions. Instructions should take the form 'Forward 5, right, forward 3, left…' and so on. If a mistake is made, the instruction 'Back' can be given.

Set the children to work in pairs on the maze exercise. One child gives instructions while the other moves a finger around the maze. Remind the children to move exactly as they have been instructed by their partner.

Differentiation
Less able children should concentrate on giving and following one instruction at a time.

Challenge more able children to write out a list of instructions for the escapee to follow. Do the listed instructions lead their partner safely to the exit?

Plenary
Conclude the lesson with a discussion of the vocabulary the children have used in their instructions. How many different ways can the children think of giving the instruction to turn right? (Turn right, clockwise 90 degrees, clockwise one quarter turn, right 90 degrees, a right angle to the right, a quarter turn to the right…)

47 Count the coins

Background

Coins are an important practical example of number groupings. Current British decimal coins group pence in twos, fives, tens, twenties, fifties, hundreds and (with the introduction of the £2 coin) two hundreds. Sorting and counting plastic 2p, 5p and 10p pieces will develop the children's counting skills. Working as a team to sort and count a large number of coins, in the context of a market stall role-play, will also develop the children's communication and teamwork skills and their use of the vocabulary of money in 'real-life' interactions.

Preparation

Set out trays filled with a variety of plastic coins on the tables for each group to count.

Main teaching activity

Start the lesson by showing the children some real coins and discussing their relative values. Match equivalent piles of plastic coins – for example, ten 1p pieces, five 2p pieces, two 5p pieces and one 10p piece. Count out a pile of ten of each type of coin, then compare the values of the different piles.

Explain that the children's task is to work together to sort and count the coins in the trays. They should imagine that they are market stall traders 'cashing up' at the end of the day. Let them tip out the coins onto the table and sort them according to their

values. They should stack the coins in piles, then count them in ones, twos, fives or tens (as appropriate) to find the value of each pile. Encourage the children to divide up the task, planning who should sort and count each type of coin. They should organise their piles of coins systematically on the table, and finally record the total value of their coins on the board.

Differentiation

Encourage more able children to experiment with different ways of grouping the coins to speed up the counting process. For example, they could sort 5p pieces into piles of ten, each containing 50p, then group the piles in twos to make pounds.
Less able children should take enough time to check carefully that their totals are accurate.

Plenary

As a class, look to see how each group has sorted its coins. Ask representatives to explain how they organised the task and divided the coins into different piles. Check their overall totals.

Linked to
Science

48 Balancing halves

Objectives

Numeracy
Begin to recognise and find one half and one quarter of shapes and small numbers of objects.
Begin to recognise that two halves or four quarters make one whole, and that two quarters and one half are equivalent.
Science
Make and record observations and measurements.
Make simple comparisons and identify simple patterns or associations...

Resources

A large classroom beam balance; a small bucket of play sand; a number of identical objects (such as unit cubes or building bricks) to count and balance.

Vocabulary

part
equal parts
fraction
one whole
one half
two halves
one quarter, two... three... four quarters

Background

As well as talking about a fraction of a whole, we can talk about a fraction of a group or a number of objects: 'Half the class are girls', 'One quarter of the shapes are triangles' and so on. This use of fractions can be introduced by dividing or sharing sets of objects equally to find one half, then one quarter. As children make these divisions, they will begin to learn the relationship between halving and doubling numbers. A quantity of sand can be accurately divided in half using a simple beam balance. The sand is distributed between the two pans and small quantities transferred until the balance is level. The quantities in the two pans are then equal. This activity links closely with science work involving the measurement of mass.

Preparation

Set up the balance in an area of the classroom where you can demonstrate its use to the whole class, then let groups take turns to use it for their investigations.

Main teaching activity

Set out a group of four objects. Explain that you wish to divide the set in half. Demonstrate that this produces two equal sets, each containing two objects. Divide each half in half again to make four quarters. Summarise by stating that half of 4 is 2 and half of 2 is 1. Ask: *How much is one quarter of 4?* Repeat the exercise with a starting set of eight objects.

Now show the class a small bucket of sand. *Can you suggest how to divide the sand accurately in half?* Demonstrate the procedure with the beam balance. Set the children working in groups at their tables to investigate the division of numbers up to 20 into halves and quarters, using objects such as unit cubes or building bricks. *Which numbers can be divided in half? Which numbers cannot be divided in half? Which numbers can be divided into quarters?* Groups can take turns to use the beam balance with their bricks, and then with the sand, to find halves and quarters.

Differentiation

Less able children should concentrate on dividing numbers to 20 in half.

More able children can be challenged to find a quarter and three-quarters of various numbers, and to devise a method for finding a quarter and three-quarters of a quantity of sand.

Plenary

Discuss the children's methods and results. They should have discovered that an even number of objects can be divided into equal halves, but an odd number cannot. To be divisible into quarters, the halves of a set of objects must also be even numbers. A set of 4, 8 or 12 objects can be quartered, but a set of 6, 10 or 14 cannot.

49 Top 10

Objectives

Numeracy
Solve a given problem by sorting, classifying and organising information in a list or simple table.

Music
Use their voices expressively by singing songs and speaking chants and rhymes.

Resources
A copy of photocopiable page 173 for each child; sample 'Top Ten' charts from magazines or supermarket posters.

Vocabulary
order
vote
table
chart
count
sort
first, second, third...

Background
In shops and supermarkets, children will see charts and displays such as *Top 10 Children's Videos, Top 50 CDs* and *Top 20 Children's Books*. Sample charts based on data collected over a period of several weeks provide an opportunity for some maths work: *Which is higher in the charts, Title A or Title B? How many places has Title C risen?* In this lesson, the children use data-handling skills to compile their own 'Top 10' chart of songs they sing at school. At the same time, they practise singing a range of popular songs.

Preparation
Distribute copies of page 173 in advance of the lesson.

Main teaching activity
Introduce the lesson by discussing 'Top 10' and similar charts. If you have brought any examples of such charts into the classroom, use these as a basis for mathematical questions – for example: *Which song is currently in seventh place? How many places is the Westlife song below the Ash song?*

With the children's help, make a list of songs sung at school on the board. Sing a verse or chorus of each song as you compile the list. Conduct a quick survey, asking the children all to vote for their favourite song. Record the

number of votes by each song title. The children should now compile a 'Top 10' list in the table on the photocopiable sheet, listing the songs in order of popularity with the most popular at number 1.

Differentiation
Less able children should concentrate on the 'Top 10' song survey.

More able children could extend the activity with class or school surveys of other 'top tens' – for example, cartoon shows, books, pets or wild animals.

Plenary
Review the 'Top 10' lists that the children have compiled. Base some quick-fire questions on the positions of the various songs and the votes received for them. *How many more votes did song A receive than song B? Did song A receive more votes than songs B and C put together?* Conclude by singing the number 1 song in the children's 'Top 10' chart.

50 Assessment 3

Objectives

The assessment activities in this book are designed to introduce Key Stage 1 children to SAT-style questions. They are set in cross-curricular contexts based on the preceding term's lessons. The questions in Assessment 3 test the children's progress in: sequencing; recognising half and quarter turns; and dividing sets of objects into halves and quarters.

Resources

One copy per child of photocopiable page 174, pencils; a selection of different-sized books, a centimetre ruler, paper, pencils.

Preparation

Make copies of the assessment sheet in advance of the lesson. If you feel that the sheet is too 'busy', the three activities could be separated and enlarged on individual sheets.

Lesson introduction

Begin the assessment lesson by reviewing the relevant cross-curricular topics covered during the term. Remind the children of some of the projects and investigations they have undertaken, and ask them to recall and recount their work. Emphasise the mathematical content – for example, *Do you remember how we shared out the olives on the pizza?*

Main assessment activity

Distribute the sheets and ask the children to work on them individually. Guide the whole class through the questions one at a time, reading the text with them and prompting them to work out and fill in the answers. Try to make the whole activity enjoyable!

Practical activity

Ask the child to:
● measure the length of each book to the nearest centimetre with the ruler
● write the measurements on the paper provided
● use the measurements to put the books in order of size, from largest to the smallest.

Plenary

Review the answers to the questions as a class. Collect the completed question sheets to use as an aid to judging individual children's progress, and to include in your records.

The answers are:

1809	1819	1840	1845
1859	1869	1889	1890

Any line that divides the faces into two sets of five.

Any two lines that divide the hearts into four sets of three.

How many sweets?

- Can you guess the number of sweets in each jar?
- Write down your estimates, then count to check.

1.

2.

3.

4.

Measure the leaves

● Measure the length and width of each leaf in centimetres.

length =
width =

length =
width =

length =
width =

length =
width =

length =
width =

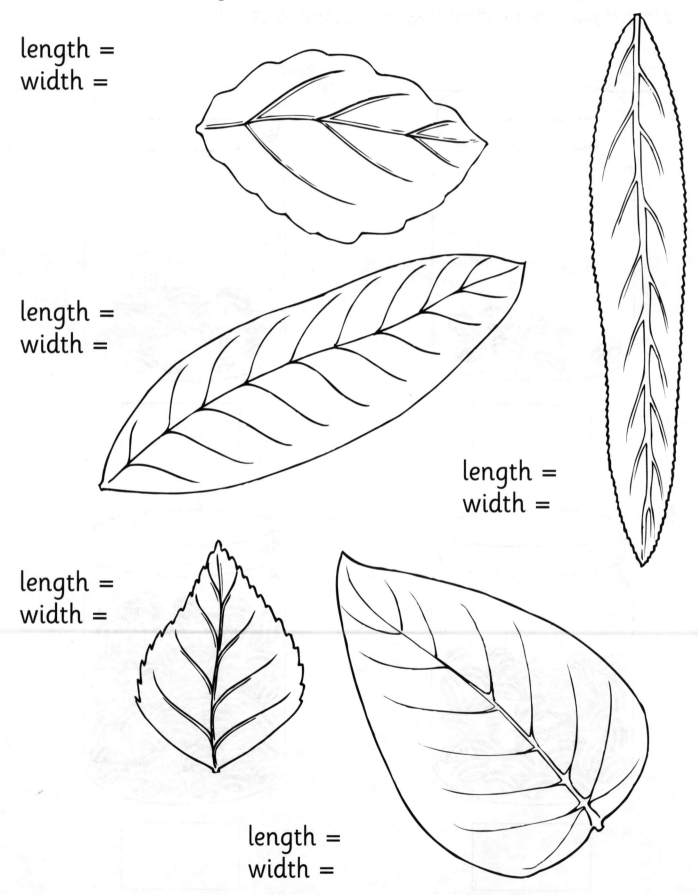

Count the bricks

● Count how many bricks there are in each wall.

Count in twos.

Count in fives.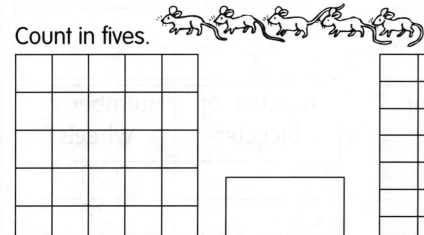

Count in tens.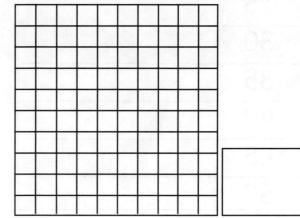

Wheels

number of bicycles	number of wheels
1	
2	
3	
4	
5	
6	
7	
8	
9	
10	

number of bicycles	number of wheels
11	
12	
13	
14	
15	
16	
17	
18	
19	
20	

number of bicycles	number of wheels
5	
10	
15	
20	
25	
30	
35	
40	
45	
50	

number of bicycles	number of wheels
	10
	20
	30
	40
	50
	60
	70
	80
	90
	100

Toy timeline

● When were these toys made?
●● Draw an arrow to join each toy to its place on the timeline.

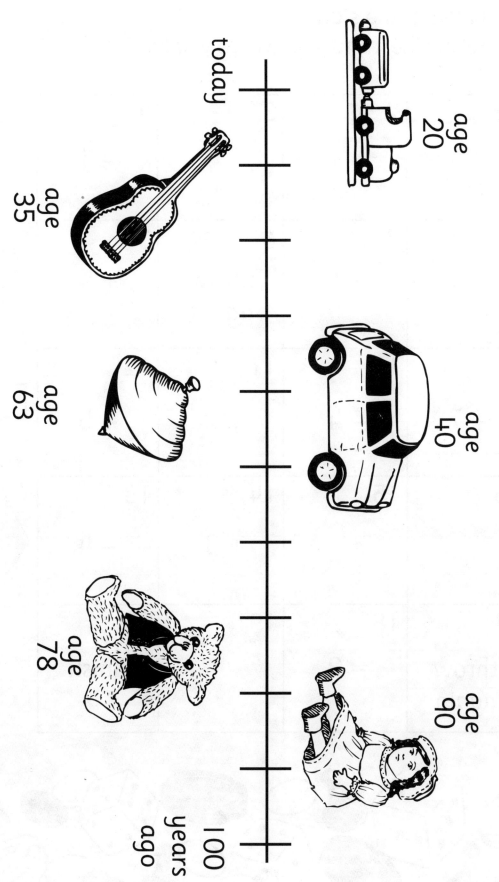

◖SCHOLASTIC

151

Board game 1

● Place your counters at the start.
  Roll the dice. Follow the instruction where you land.

0 start	1	2 + 1	3	4 − 1
8 + 3	7 − 4	6 throw again	5 + 4	
9 + 7	10 − 4	11 + 2	12 + 5	
16	15	14 + 3	13 − 4	
17 throw again	18 − 2	19	20 finish	

Board game 2

- Place your counters at the start.
- Roll the dice. Follow the instruction where you land.

0 start	1 throw again	2	3	4 +5	5	6 −3	7	8 +6	9	10 −5
20	19 +7	18	17 −2	16	15 +10	14	13 −1	12 +4	11	
21	22 −8	23	24 +1	25 throw again	26 +7	27	28 −11	29	30 +3	
40	39 +12	38 −7	37 +5	36	35 −5	34	33 +7	32	31	
41	42 +4	43	44	45 +20	46 throw again	47 −2	48 −11	49	50 +15	
60	59 throw again	58 −3	57	56 −8	55	54 −24	53 +30	52 −3	51 −6	
61 +5	62	63 −11	64	65 +21	66 throw again	67 −5	68	69 +9	70	
80	79 +12	78	77 −13	76	75 −2	74 throw again	73 +4	72	71 −6	
81	82 +5	83	84	85 +3	86	87 −21	88 throw again	89	90 −50	
100 finish	99	98	97 +2	96 −11	95 throw again	94 −4	93	92 −5	91 −10	

Story problems

● Solve these problems.

1. There are eight people in a room. Five more come in. How many people are in the room altogether?

2. A farmer has six sheep. He buys nine more. How many sheep does he have?

3. Jamie has ten cards. Sakina has six cards. If they share their cards equally, how many will they each have?

4. There are 18 people on a bus. Half of them get off. How many are left?

5. Sophie has six books. She takes two back to the library and gets four more out. How many books does she have now?

6. Rachael has 15 sweets. She gives four to Jo and six to Vimty. How many sweets does Rachael have left?

7. Shane has 14 pencils in his box. He takes out eight pencils, then puts five back. How many pencils does he have in his box now?

8. There are 11 people in a room. Five people go out and twelve more come in. How many people are in the room?

9. Karim has 25 stickers. He uses 8 on Tuesday and 11 on Wednesday. How many stickers does Karim have left?

10. Chloe has 6 buttons on her jacket, 4 buttons on her shirt and 3 buttons on her trousers. How many buttons does she have altogether?

● Write some 'story problems' of your own.

Fair shares

● Share the seaside sets fairly.

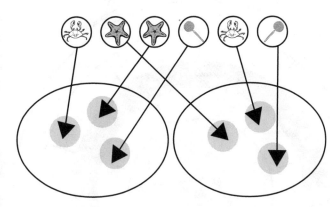

between 2

$6 \div 2 = 3$

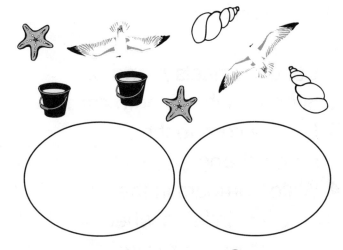

between 2

$8 \div 2 = \boxed{}$

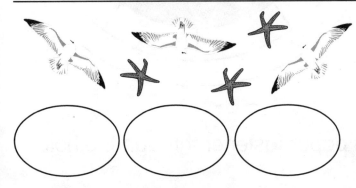

between 3

$6 \div 3 = \boxed{}$

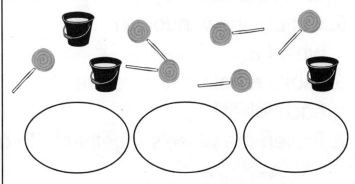

between 3

$9 \div 3 = \boxed{}$

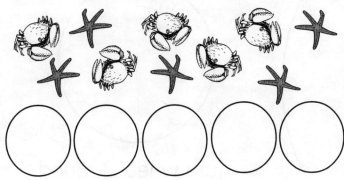

between 5

$10 \div 5 = \boxed{}$

between 5

$15 \div 5 = \boxed{}$

Doubling machine

● Instructions

1. Cut out wheels A and B.
2. Stick the wheels onto card.
3. Cut the card to the same shape.
4. Write numbers in the smaller circle on wheel A, inside the black band. Write their doubles in the larger circle, outside the black band.
5. Cut out the windows in wheel B.
6. Make a hole at the centre of each wheel.
7. Fasten the wheels together with a paper fastener through the holes.

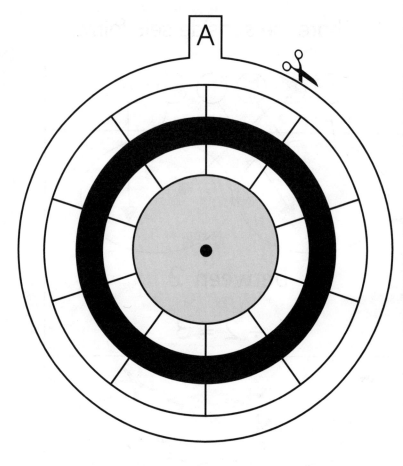

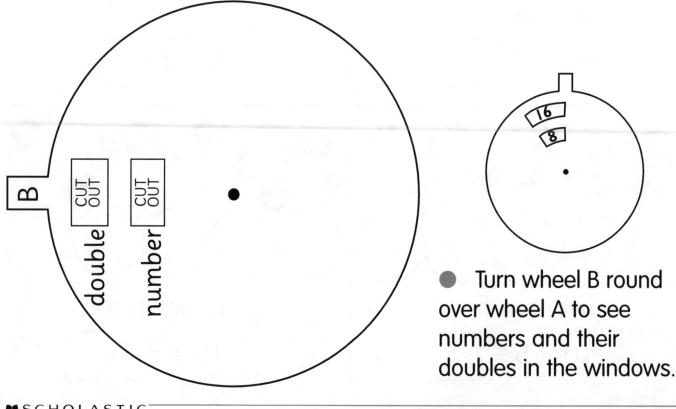

● Turn wheel B round over wheel A to see numbers and their doubles in the windows.

Champion vegetables

- Write its length on each carrot.
- Award the prizes to the longest carrots.

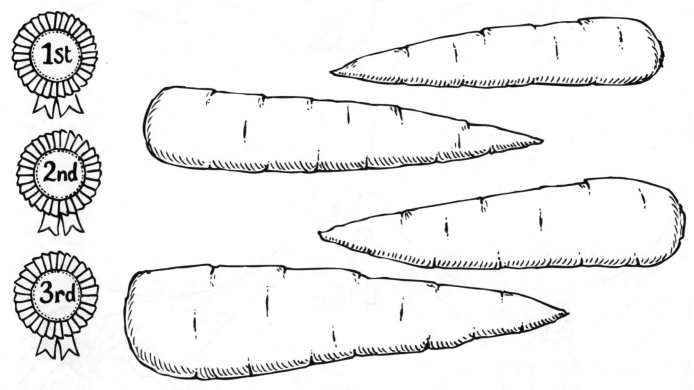

- Write its mass on each pumpkin.
- Award the prizes to the heaviest pumpkins.

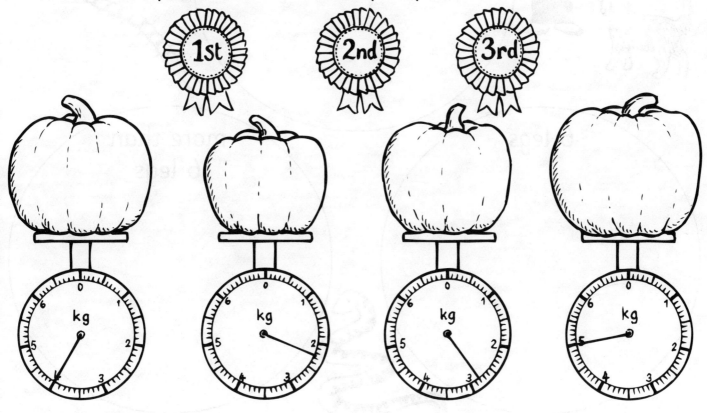

How many legs?

● Write the names of as many animals as you can in each set.

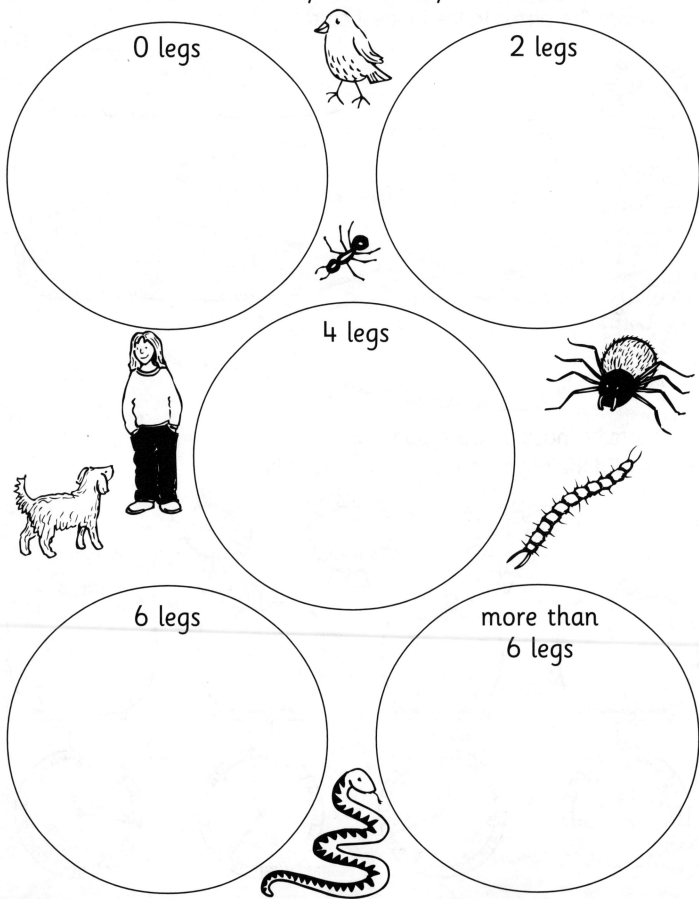

0 legs

2 legs

4 legs

6 legs

more than 6 legs

Name

● Colour odd numbers.

1	2	3	4	5
6	7	8	9	10
11	12	13	14	15
16	17	18	19	20
21	22	23	24	25

● Colour multiples of 2.

1	2	3	4	5
6	7	8	9	10
11	12	13	14	15
16	17	18	19	20
21	22	23	24	25

● Measure these leaves to the nearest cm.

length =
width =

length =
width =

● Write numbers to solve these story problems.

There are eighteen people in a room. Nine more people come in. How many people are in the room?

[   ] + [   ] = [   ]

There are thirty passengers on a bus. Twenty get off. Six more get on. How many passengers are on the bus?

[   ] − [   ] + [   ] = [   ]

Bingo!

1	12	22	32	40	51		70	84	92
4		23	34		54	63		85	94
	15	25		45		66	75	88	
9	18		36	48	59	69	78		99

	12	21	30	42		60	72	80	
3	13		33		56	62	73	84	91
5	17	26		47	57		77		96
8		29	37	48	59	67		89	97

2	10	22		40	51	63	70		93
4		25	33	43		65		82	94
5	16		35		56	69	77	88	
	19	28	39	49	58		79	89	98

1	11	21	31		53	60		80	93
		23	35	44	55		75		96
6	17		38	46		66	76	83	97
8	18	28		48	57	68	78	86	

Magic squares

● Is this a magic square?

6	4	5
4	5	6
5	6	4

● Make a magic square with 1, 1, 1, 2, 2, 2, 3, 3, 3.

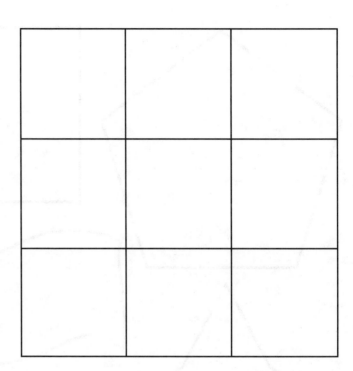

● Make a magic square with 3, 3, 3, 4, 4, 4, 5, 5, 5.

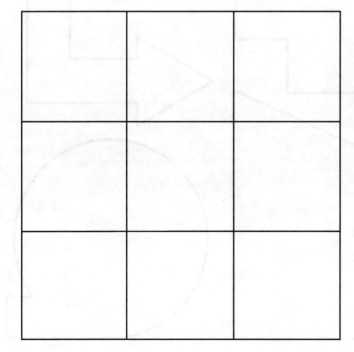

● Make a magic square with 1, 2, 3, 4, 5, 6, 7, 8, 9.

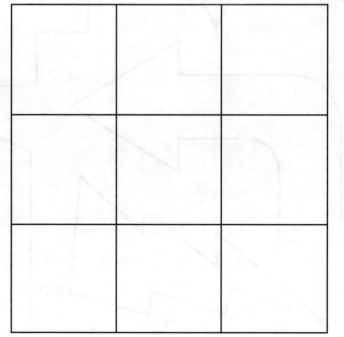

Mirror symmetry

● Which shapes are symmetrical?
Use a mirror to check.

Count the beats

1, 2

1, 2, 3

1, 2, 3, 4

1, 2, 3, 4, 5

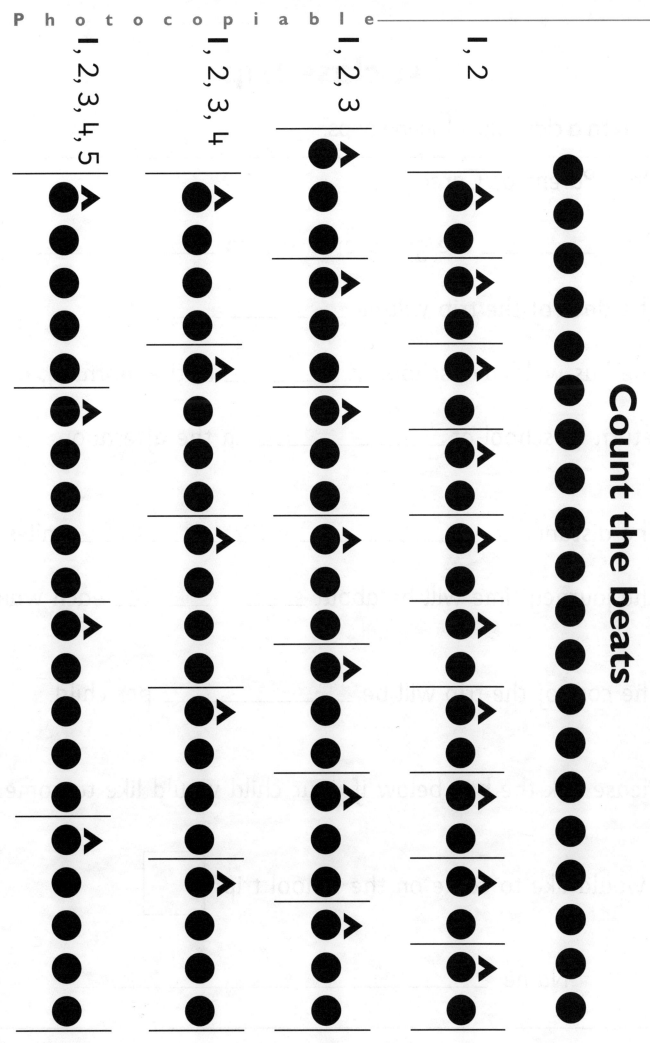

A class trip

● Plan a class trip. Fill in the gaps.

Dear Parent or Carer,

Class _____ are going on a trip to _____.

The date of the trip will be _____.

The bus will leave school at _____ in the morning, and

return to school at _____ in the afternoon.

The distance to_____ is _____ miles.

The journey time will be about _____ each way.

The cost of the trip will be _____ per child.

Please tick the box below if your child would like to come.

I would like to come on the school trip. [ ]

Name: _____

Fruit fractions

● Cut these fruits into halves.

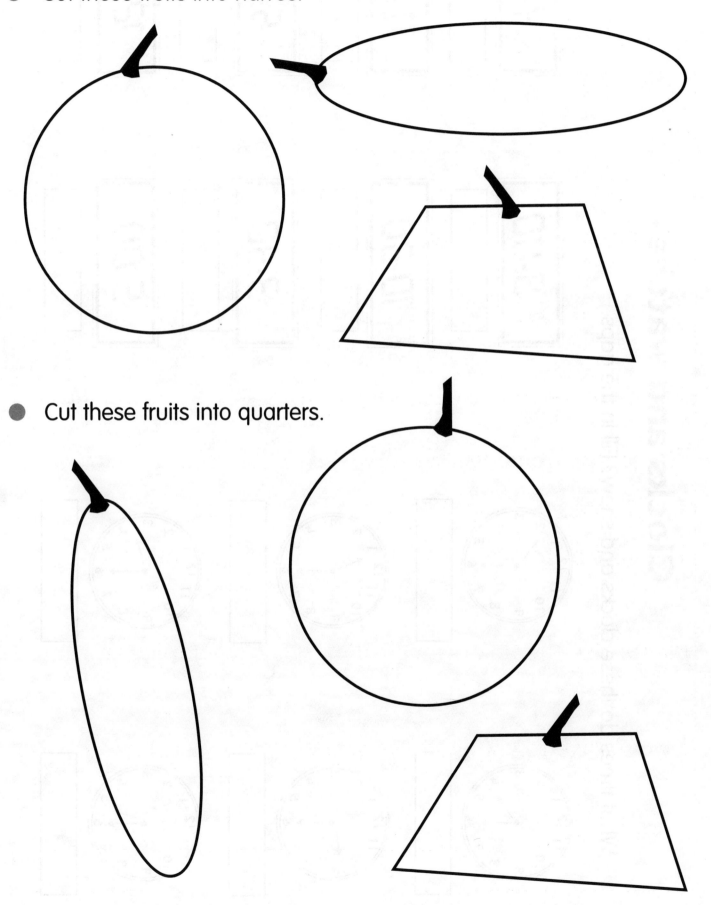

● Cut these fruits into quarters.

Clocks and watches

What times do these clocks and show? Fill in the gaps.

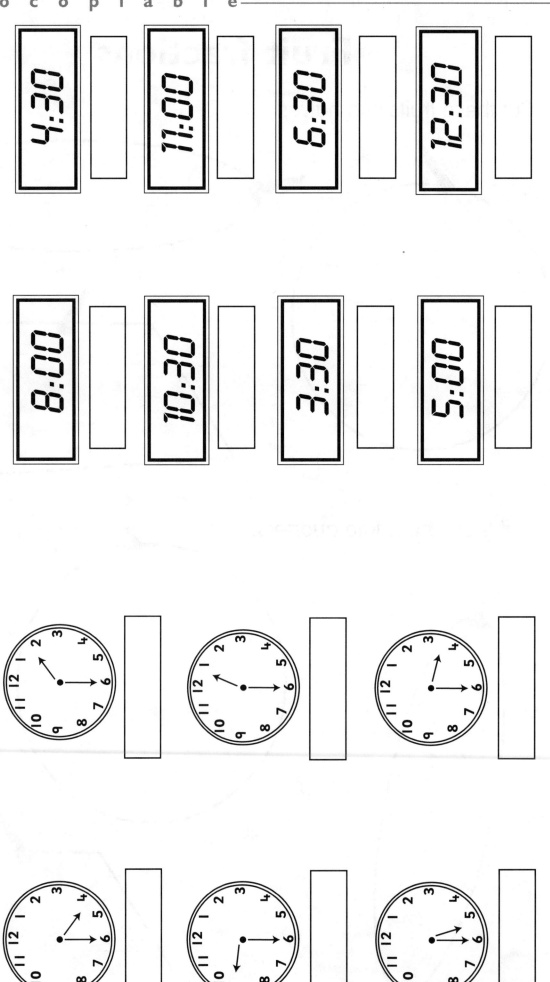

Name

- Write these numbers on the Bingo card:

99, 13, 45, 91, 2, 33, 74, 66,
85, 34, 82, 8, 24, 58, 96, 29, 68

	12	21		42		60	72		
					56				
5	17						77		
			37	48	59			89	

- Use these numbers to complete the magic square:

2, 4, 6, 8

	7	
9	5	1
	3	

- Match the shapes and names.

   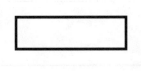 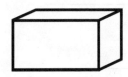

square   triangle   rectangle   pentagon   hexagon   circle

sphere   cone   cylinder   cube   cuboid

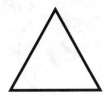 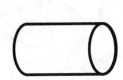  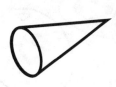 

Number words and numerals

● Write the numerals.

nineteen _____   twenty-seven _____

fifty-four _____   seventeen _____

seventy-six _____   thirty-eight _____

ninety-two _____   eighty-five _____

forty-seven _____   twenty-one _____

● Write the number words.

16 _____   11 _____

24 _____   33 _____

62 _____   49 _____

58 _____   99 _____

86 _____   71 _____

Months and seasons

● Write the names of the months and seasons in the correct order.

Seasons

Months

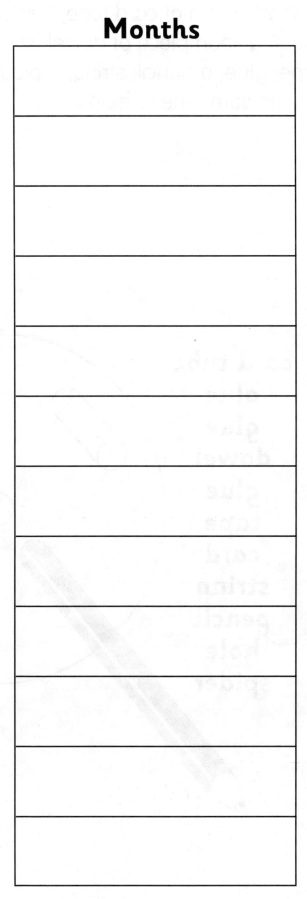

Wind it up

You will need:
a short length of card tube, two card discs, a short piece of dowel, sticky tape, glue, a pencil, string, a plastic spider, someone to help.

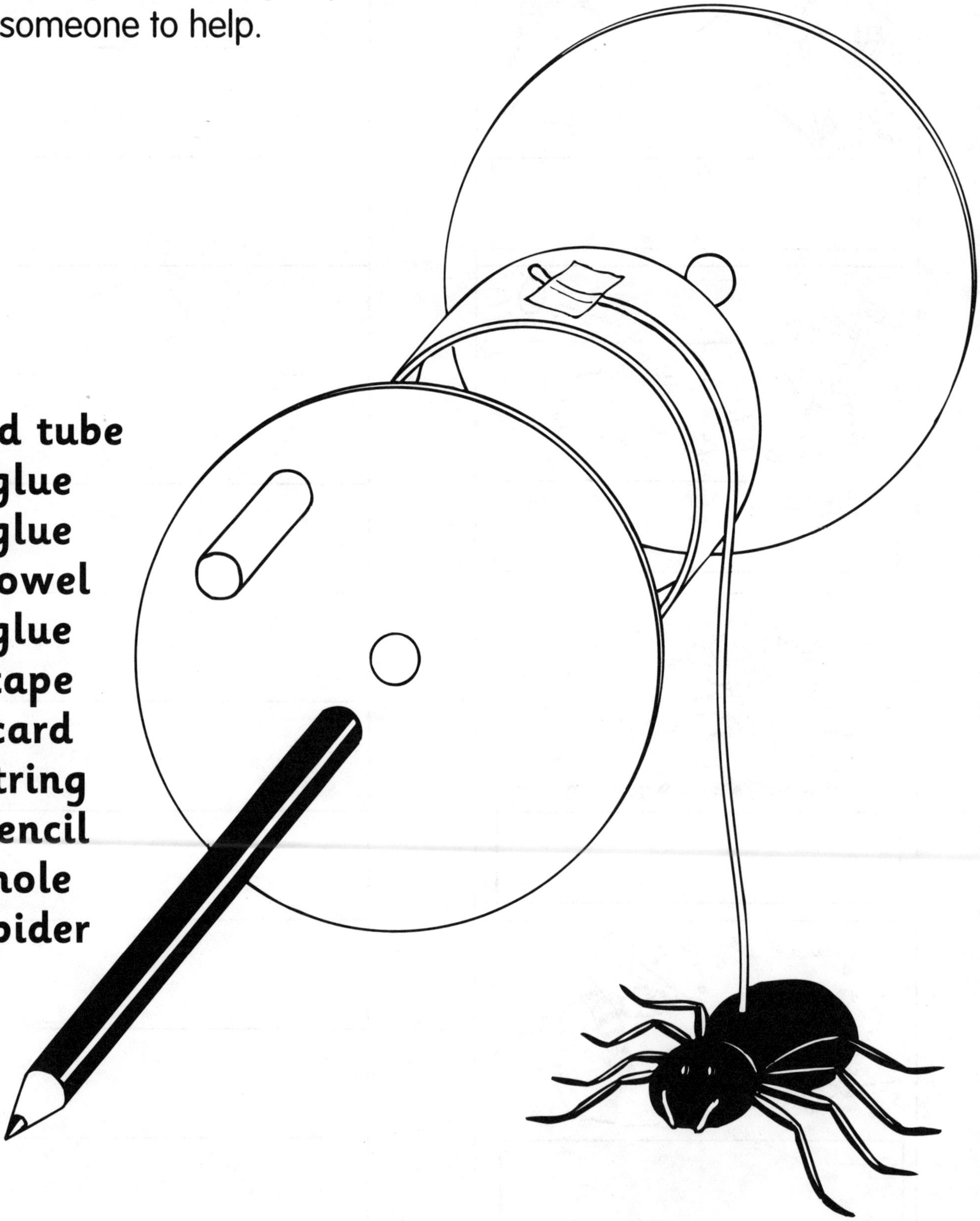

card tube
glue
glue
dowel
glue
tape
card
string
pencil
hole
spider

Florence Nightingale 1820–1910

Age 40 Founded school for nurses.	Age 36 Returned to England.	Age 90 Died.	Age 31 Went to Germany by train.	Age 17 Felt called by God to do special work.	Age 25 Decided to nurse the sick.	Age 34 Went to the Crimea to nurse soldiers.

Year

1820 1830 1840 1850 1860 1870 1880 1890 1900 1910 1920

0 10 20 30 40 50 60 70 80 90

Florence's age in years

Maze masters

● Give instructions to help your friend escape from the mazes.
● Take care not to let your friend meet a Minotaur!

Top 10

Place		Votes
1		
2		
3		
4		
5		
6		
7		
8		
9		
10		

Name

● Write these years in the correct order.

1890   1809   1859   1819   1889   1845   1840   1869

● Which way must you turn the handle to wind the spider up?

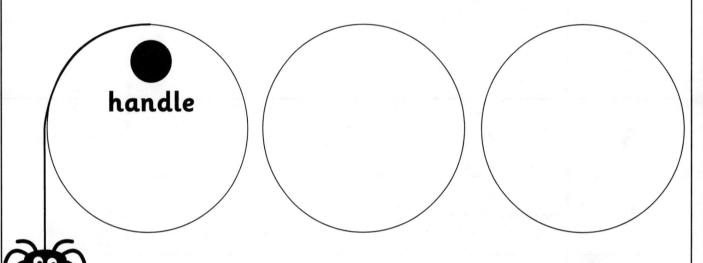

handle

Draw an arrow on the handle.

Draw the handle after a half turn.

Draw the handle after another quarter turn.

● Draw a line to divide this set in half.

● Draw two lines to divide this set in quarters.